At Issue

Teen Suicide

Other Books in the At Issue Series:

At Issue

Teen Suicide

Emily Schusterbauer, Book Editor

GREENHAVEN PRESS
A part of Gale, Cengage Learning

GALE
CENGAGE Learning

Detroit • New York • San Francisco • New Haven, Conn • Waterville, Maine • London

Christine Nasso, *Publisher*
Elizabeth Des Chenes, *Managing Editor*

© 2009 Greenhaven Press, a part of Gale, Cengage Learning.

Gale and Greenhaven Press are registered trademarks used herein under license.

For more information, contact:
Greenhaven Press
27500 Drake Rd.
Farmington Hills, MI 48331-3535
Or you can visit our Internet site at gale.cengage.com

For product information and technology assistance, contact us at

Gale Customer Support, 1-800-877-4253
For permission to use material from this text or product, submit all requests online at
www.cengage.com/permissions

Further permissions questions can be emailed to permissionrequest@cengage.com

Articles in Greenhaven Press anthologies are often edited for length to meet page requirements. In addition, original titles of these works are changed to clearly present the main thesis and to explicitly indicate the author's opinion. Every effort is made to ensure that Greenhaven Press accurately reflects the original intent of the authors. Every effort has been made to trace the owners of copyrighted material.

Cover photograph © Images.com/Corbis.

LIBRARY OF CONGRESS CATALOGING-IN-PUBLICATION DATA

Teen suicide / Emily Schusterbauer, book editor.
        p. cm. -- (At issue)
    Includes bibliographical references and index.
    ISBN 978-0-7377-4418-7 (hardcover)
    ISBN 978-0-7377-4419-4 (pbk.)
    1. Teenagers--Suicidal behavior--United States. 2. Teenagers--Mental health--United States. 3. Depression in adolescence--United States. 4. Adolescent psychology--United States. I. Schusterbauer, Emily.
    HV6546.T4138 2009
    362.280835--dc22
                                                            2008055845

Printed in the United States of America
    2 3 4 5 6   13 12 11 10 09

ED217

Contents

Introduction

The question of whether nonheterosexual identity constitutes a risk factor for teen suicide has generated considerable attention and concern. This question is particularly complex because in order to answer it, researchers must consider both the complexities of adolescent identity and the complexities of sexual identity. General risk factors, faced by both heterosexual and homosexual teens, must be controlled for, and the distinction between homosexual sex acts and homosexual identity must be considered. Potential differences between and among gay, lesbian, and bisexual teenagers must be recognized. And, because of this, even studies indicating a significant connection between homosexual identity and increased adolescent suicide risk should be carefully interpreted.

In 2003, in the *Journal of Abnormal Psychology*, Lars Wichstrom and Kristinn Hegna published the results of a seven-year study aimed at assessing adolescent suicide risk among gay, lesbian, and bisexual Norwegians in seventh through twelfth grade. Throughout their article, titled "Sexual Orientation and Suicide Attempt: A Longitudinal Study of the General Norwegian Adolescent Population," Wichstrom and Hegna both liken their research to, and distinguished it from, past work on the issue of nonheterosexual teen suicide. At the very outset of their text, they note that "several recent studies of probability samples all suggest that gay, lesbian, and bisexual (GLB) young people are at greater risk for self-reported attempted suicide than heterosexual young people." They go on, however, to assert that "a series of important questions still remain unanswered." In particular, Wichstrom and Hegna suggest that previous research indicating increased suicide risk among gay, lesbian, and bisexual teens neither grappled with the complex nature of sexual identity nor controlled for the known suicide risk factors of early sexual maturation and early sexual debut. In their study, therefore, Wichstrom and Hegna expanded the number of risk factors controlled for—paying particular attention to those risk factors most often reported by gay, lesbian, and bisexual teens—and distinguished between nonheterosexual desire, nonheterosexual activity, and nonheterosexual identity. Finally, Wichstrom and Hegna's longitudinal study design allowed them to measure both past and future suicidality among their study population. Unlike other studies, which measured suicidal thoughts and suicide attempts only retrospectively, asking participants if they *had* ever considered or attempted suicide, Wichstrom and Hegna were able to track the suicidal thoughts and behaviors that developed in their participants after their initial rounds of data collection.

Thus, Wichstrom and Hegna report their primary finding, that adolescents who have engaged in same-sex sexual contact face increased suicide risk, in a fair amount of detail and with a fair amount of confidence. Distinguishing between homosexual identities and homosexual acts, and marking gender as a significant category of analysis, Wichstrom and Hegna report that, while "same-sex contact was associated with increased odds of previous suicide attempts [among all participants] . . . same-sex sexual contact was associated with increased odds for a future suicide attempt among girls but not among boys." Although they admit that their study faced certain limitations, mostly due to an inability to follow all participants from the first data collection in 1992 through the final date collection in 1999, Wichstrom and Hegna nonetheless frame their work as more nuanced than previous work addressing the same topic. And, yet, Wichstrom and Hegna's findings are called into question by Elizabeth Saewyc in her 2007 article titled "Contested Conclusions: Claims That Can (and Cannot) Be Made from the Current Research on Gay, Lesbian, and Bisexual Teen Suicide Attempts." For while Saewyc acknowledges the usefulness of Wichstrom and Hegna's longitudinal study design, she sees their work as symptomatic of a larger problem in studies assessing the connection between gay, lesbian and bisexual identity and adolescent suicide risk. Specifically, Saewyc interprets Wichstrom and Hegna, and the many researchers with whom they are in conversation, as too easily assuming that connections indicate causal links or too easily concluding that same-sex sexual contact *itself* causes elevated suicide rates among gay, lesbian, and bisexual teens. Noting that "few research designs can even come close to 'proving' cause and effect," and arguing that "those [research designs] that more strongly suggest causal links between risk factors and outcomes may be impossible or unethical for public health research to use," Saewyc is more critical of Wichstrom and Hegna's conclusions than of their methodology. Although Saewyc points out that Wichstrom and Hegna do not adequately control for coercive sexual experiences and school harassment and victimization as risk factors, this is not her primary point of criticism. Rather, Saewyc simply contends that same-sex sexual contact should not, itself, be interpreted as a risk factor for adolescent suicidality. In no uncertain terms, she writes that "since no reported suicide attempt rates among LGB youth are anywhere near 100%, we can rule out being LGB as a 'cause' of suicide."

Here, what comes to light is not the inadequacy of a specific research model or the unimportance of a specific research agenda but rather the difficulty of isolating any single experience or identity category in order to assess its relationship to adolescent suicide risk. Although sexuality might be particularly hard to study because of its fluid categories and definitions, researchers studying the relationship between gay, lesbian, and bisexual identity and teen suicidality contend with the same uncertainties with which any researcher studying adolescent suicidality must contend. From this interface between Wichstrom and Hegna and Saewyc there arises the warning that risk factors are largely interconnected and causal relationships largely elusive. While simply tragic in its ramifications and its frequency, adolescent suicide may be more complex than singular risk factors would suggest. Why certain teens commit suicide is a question that can escape even the most rigorous research agendas. Researchers, however, will no doubt continue to prove the causes in an effort to identify adolescents that may be at higher risk.

1

Teen Suicide Myths Hamper Preventive Efforts

Michelle Ann Moskos, Jennifer Achilles, and Doug Gray

Michelle Ann Moskos is a consulting epidemiologist for the Utah Department of Health, the American Association of Suicidology, and the National Suicide Prevention Resource Center. Jennifer Achilles served as the study coordinator of the Utah Youth Suicide Study. Doug Gray is a child and developmental psychiatrist and and assistant professor of psychiatry at the University of Utah School of Medicine.

Since the 1990s, attempts to study, treat, and prevent adolescent suicide have become increasingly common. Recognized as a significant issue that continually affects young people and their families, adolescent suicide has taken center stage in much psychological and psychiatric research and has gained the attention of the U.S. surgeon general's office. Still, empirical data reflecting the reality of who commits suicide and why is often lacking. In place of such data, myths about adolescent suicide abound. Ultimately, these myths impede efforts to effectively address the very real problem of teen suicide.

The prevention of violence, in particular, suicide, is of international concern. In 1999, the United States Surgeon General issued a Call to Action to Prevent Suicide because the most current statistics identified suicide as the ninth leading cause of mortality in the United States with nearly 31,000 deaths. Concomitantly, the World Health Organization (WHO) recognized suicide as a growing problem worldwide with nearly 1,000,000 deaths and urged member nations to take action. The WHO document, *Prevention of Suicide: Guidelines for the Formulation and Implementation of National Strategies*, motivated a partnership to seek a national strategy in the United States. In 2001, the United States Surgeon General released the *National Strategy for Suicide Prevention: Goals and Objectives for Action*, which is a plan that will guide the nation's suicide prevention efforts for the next ten years. This document provides essential guidance and suggests the fundamental activities that must follow—activities based on scientific evidence. The National Strategy emphasized that, "much of the work of suicide prevention must occur at the community level where human relationships breathe life into public policy." In 2002, the Institute of Medicine (IOM) released *Reducing Suicide: A National Imperative*. The IOM clarifies the medical, social, psychological, economic, moral, and political facets of suicide and the need for prevention. Teen suicide rates tripled over several decades in the United States, but have declined slightly since the mid-1990s. Suicide, by its nature, is a complex problem. Many myths have developed about individuals who complete suicide, suicide risk factors, current prevention programs, and the treatment of at-risk youth in the United States. There are certain myths that suicidologists encounter in their work with the general population, health professionals, school administrators, and other government officials, as well as the media. The purpose of this article is to address these myths related to suicide in the United States, to separate fact from fiction, and offer recommendations for future suicide prevention programs.

Myth #1: Suicide Attempters and Completers Are Similar

The epidemiology of suicide attempts and completions vary internationally. In the United States, males are four times more likely to die from suicide than females, but females are more likely to attempt suicide than males. In 1999, 83% of teenage suicide completers were male. The only statewide hospital surveillance study of child and adolescent suicide attempters in the United States demonstrated that 84% of attempters were female. Suicide attempts peak in the teenage years, while suicide completion peaks in old age. The United States does not have an official source that compiles suicide-attempt data nationwide, therefore, reported rates are speculative. However, the average estimated ratio between nonfatal youth suicide attempters and youth suicide completers in the United States was 100–200:1. In a smaller study, researchers found that adolescent suicide attempters are a large group, with a 1 year incidence rate of 130/100,000 suicide attempts among those with no baseline suicidal behaviors. By contrast suicide completion is a rare event, involving only 1–2/10,000 teenagers each year. While suicide attempts increase the long-term risk of suicide, the majority of teen suicide completers have never made a prior attempt. Gender differences can be explained by the choice of more lethal means by males, and by cultural influences making it more acceptable for males to complete rather than attempt suicide.

In the United States, males are four times more likely to die from suicide than females, but females are more likely to attempt suicide than males.

Recommendations

It will be important to recognize that suicide attempters and completers are two different groups, with some overlap. These two groups will require separate treatment interventions, and outcome measures specific to each group. Cultural influences must also be addressed.

Myth #2: Current Prevention Programs Work

National suicide prevention efforts have focused on school education programs, teen suicide hotlines, media guidelines, and efforts to limit firearm access for at-risk youth. Unfortunately, these prevention methods have not had a significant impact in lowering teen suicide rates. Historically, suicide prevention programs have not been rigorously evaluated, and, consequently, resources have not been focused on high-risk groups. School-based suicide prevention programs have not been demonstrated to effect suicide rates, and educational benefits have been limited to a few studies. In 2004, an evaluation of Signs of Suicide (SOS), a school-based suicide prevention program, documented a reduction in self-reported suicide attempts for the first time using a randomized experimental design. This study was unique, because it incorporated screening and referral of high-risk youth in addition to an educational component. Teen hotlines are primarily used by females, rather than males, thus having little effect on the group with the highest risk for death. Approximately 5% of all teen suicides are believed to be "cluster" suicides. Cluster suicides involve additional imitative suicides, based on the idea of a contagion, which may be associated with the way the media describe suicide. The Centers for Disease Control and Prevention (CDC) have developed guidelines for the reporting of suicide in the media in the United States. Because the implementation of similar recommendations for media coverage of suicide has been shown to decrease suicide rates in Europe, we strongly support the use of the CDC guidelines for media in the United States, although their effectiveness warrants examination. There is general agreement that reducing access to lethal means can reduce suicide completion rates, in fact, according to the CDC, restricting access to lethal means may be one of the most promising underused strategies that warrant further examination. Unfortunately, a recent study demonstrated that only 25% of gun owners remove firearms from their home when repeatedly asked to do so by their teenager's mental health provider. In Canada, [A.] Leenaars and colleagues explored the relationship between Canada's Criminal Law Amendment Act of 1977 and Canadian suicide rates; although legislative gun control correlated with a decrease in suicide rates, this approach is probably unfeasible in the United States.

Adolescent and young adult suicide rates have more than tripled between the 1960s and 1990s.

Recommendations

Suicidologists recommend that future efforts in the educational system use evidence-based screening tools to identify youth at risk, and link screening responses to appropriate treatment referrals. Limitations include the cost of screening tools used in school settings, as well as the number of false positives. Educational programs which consist only of a brief, one-time lecture regarding risk factors for youth suicide have not been effective. Teen hotlines may be effective in helping suicide attempters. An appropriate outcome measure for hotlines could be a reduction in the number of emergency room visits for suicide attempts rather than a reduction in the number of suicide deaths. Reducing access to lethal means may require health professionals to change their strategy of encouraging the removal of firearms to encouraging the safe storage of firearms. Data from the Utah Youth Suicide Study by Gray and colleagues (2002) indicated that the Juvenile Justice System provides a unique opportunity to identify youth at risk for suicide. The study found that 63% of youth suicide completers had contact with Juvenile Justice, usually multiple minor offenses over many years. Less than half (46%) of the youths found in the justice system could also be located in the public educational system. This finding suggests that mental health screening and treatment should be integrated into the nation's Juvenile Justice systems.

Myth #3: Teens Have the Highest Suicide Rate

In the United States, elderly white males have always had the highest risk for completed suicide. Often suicide in the geriatric population is related to a medical disability. However, older adult suicide rates have stayed relatively constant in the United States, while adolescent and young adult suicide rates have more than tripled between the 1960s and 1990s. The CDC considers years of potential life lost (YPLL) to gauge the impact of an illness on a population. Teen suicide involves considerable YPLL, and for teenagers nationwide, suicide is one of the leading causes of death. In addition, cluster suicides predominately occur in the teenage population. Rates of suicide among minorities are low compared to whites. The rate of suicide among African American youth in the United States is increasing faster than any other ethnic group. Surprisingly, the rise in African American youth suicide in the United States is concentrated in those with higher socioeconomic status.

Recommendations

Future prevention efforts should continue to be focused on adolescents and young adults, given the social, economic, and emotional impact of youth suicide. While the white population has had the highest suicide rates, other ethnic groups need greater consideration, because of changing epidemiology.

Myth #4: Suicide Is Caused by Family and Social Stress

When interviewing families of suicide victims, relatives often point to an adverse precipitant, such as breaking off a romantic relationship, an argument with parents, or a disciplinary action. One feature of adolescent suicide is that it may be precipitated by a psycho-social stressor associated with a recent loss, rejection, or disciplinary crisis. However, stressors related to these events are common in a normal teenager's life, and suicide is a rare outcome. Studies have shown that over 90% of teen suicide completers have psychiatric diagnoses, most commonly a mood disorder with comorbid substance abuse or conduct problems. Teens who complete suicide have more stress and family dysfunction. However, we know that mental illness runs in families, and either child psychopathology or parental psychopathology may account for stressors related to family dysfunction. For example, [A.] Brent found that parent-child discord was associated with adolescent suicide, yet when this study controlled for proband psychopathology, parent-child discord made no significant contribution. The largest controlled studies conducted to date come to different conclusions regarding negative interactions between victims and their parents, and whether history of severe physical punishment plays a role in youth suicide. While suicide victims are more likely to come from nonintact families, the overall effect of divorce on suicide risk is small. While 19% of youth suicide completers in Utah had been reported to Child Protective Services, most reports involved teenagers having physical altercations with their parents, rather than abuse or neglect of small children. The available information leads to the question of whether the family dysfunction contributes to mental illness, or whether the mental illness contributes to the family dysfunction. Separate from family dysfunction, both child and parent psychopathology have been associated with an increased risk for suicide in Denmark.

Recommendations

Suicide "is caused" by an interplay of biological, psychological, environmental, and social factors. However, it is essential to screen, identify, and treat mental illness in teenagers, because mental illness is a known risk factor for suicide. Furthermore, the identification and referral for mental health treatment of any psychopathology in parents of teenagers at risk for suicide is needed. Treating either child or parental psychopathology, or both, should decrease both parent-child discord and family dysfunction.

National studies indicate that very few suicide completers were in treatment at the time of their death.

Myth #5: Suicide Is Not Inherited

Genetics has a critical role in mental illness and suicide. If an individual who is adopted at birth completes suicide, it is their biological relatives who are at increased risk for suicide, not the adoptive family members. Suicide rates are higher among monozygotic [identical] twins, compared with dizygotic [fraternal] twins. The genetics of suicide are complex. For example, some families are at increased risk for depression over multiple generations, while other families have increased risk for both depression and suicide. Perhaps the later families inherit a more virulent form of depression? A study in Denmark confirmed that youth are more likely to commit suicide if they had a family history of mental illness or they had been diagnosed with a mental illness; however, no one psychiatric diagnosis versus another in parents was associated with an increased risk for suicide among their children. Brent raises the possibility of a two-factor genetic model, where a patient must inherit both a mental illness, and a second factor, such as impulsivity/aggression.

Recommendations

Future suicide prevention efforts need to focus on identifying a phenotype [an observable characteristic] that predisposes to suicide. A more specific phenotype will help us to identify individuals at risk. Clarifying the phenotype is an integral step in discovering the genetic basis of suicide, because it is unknown whether risk for suicide is mediated by a history of mental illness in the family or the presence of a phenotype that could be associated with either suicide or mental illness, or both.

Too often suicide prevention programs do not use evidence-based research or practice methodologies. More funding is warranted to continue evidence-based studies in suicide.

Myth #6: Teen Suicide Represents Treatment Failure

National studies indicate that very few suicide completers were in treatment at the time of their death. According to [A.] Gray and colleagues, government agency data revealed that only 1% of youth suicide completers were in public mental health treatment at the time of their suicide, and only 3% of youth suicide completers had detectable levels of psychotropic medication in their blood sample at autopsy. From 1952–1995, the incidence of suicide among adolescents nearly tripled; however, rates began to level off in the mid 1990s, and are beginning to decline. Interestingly, this change in suicide rate coincides with the rapid increase in use of antidepressants and mood stabilizers in children and adolescents. In Sweden, there was a 25% reduction in the overall suicide rate, which accompanied a four-fold increase in antidepressant use. While there is no proof of a causal relationship between the use of antidepressants or mood stabilizers and a decrease in suicide completion, other known factors affecting suicide completion rates such as divorce or substance abuse were unchanged. [M.] Moskos and colleagues conducted a study of parent and community contacts of teen suicide completers and found that a lack of appropriate treatment, or compliance with treatment (i.e., use of psychotropic medications) for mental illness, leads to suicide completion rather than mental illness alone. Additionally, parents identified the stigma of mental illness and the denial of mental illness as the most significant barriers between teen suicide completers and treatment. More recently, a study by [M.] Olfson and colleagues examined the relationship between regional changes in antidepressant medication treatment and suicide rates in the United States, and reported a relationship between increased antidepressant use and decreased suicide rates, especially among teenage males. Psychotropic medications can ameliorate symptoms, reduce disability, shorten the course of several psychological disorders, and prevent relapse. However, in the United States and Finland, while there has been a several fold increase in antidepressant use in the general population, most individuals with major depression remain untreated. Undertreatment is more prevalent among children and adolescents than young adults. A limiting factor in treating psychiatric disorders is the lack of psychopharmacologic studies with children and adolescents. While some psychotropic medications (i.e., antidepressants) have FDA- [Food and Drug Administration-]approved uses in the pediatric population, many medications approved for adults are yet to receive adequate trials in younger age groups. The lack of empirically-based studies, which exist but were not made public due to proprietary issues, has led to some controversy regarding the use of certain Selective Serotonin Reuptake Inhibitors (SSRIs) to treat depression in children and adolescents.

Recommendations

The association between the increase of antidepressant use and decrease of suicide rates warrants further examination. We recommend government intervention to require pharmaceutical companies to study new psychotropic medications in pediatric populations, and to inform the public of their findings before these drags come to public market. More research into biological and psychosocial aspects of mental health is necessary to increase the understanding of the cause, course, and outcomes of mental illness and to develop more effective treatment options. We also recommend that all pediatric psychopharmacologic studies be published, including studies with negative results. Public awareness of the available treatments for psychiatric disorders is vital. It may not be the mental illness itself, but rather the lack of treatment or compliance with treatment, which may lead to suicide completion. Barriers to treatment for mental illness must be addressed if the teen suicide rate is to be reduced. These include denial of mental illness, stigma, mental health insurance parity, and other barriers. Public awareness can reduce the stigma of both the diagnosis and treatment of mental illness.

More Accurate Knowledge Needed

Unfortunately, the six myths of teen suicide outlined above indicate that evidence-based information is still needed to combat the high teen suicide rate in the United States. Psychiatric illnesses are often viewed differently from other medical problems. Research should precede any public health effort, so that prevention programs can be designed, implemented, and evaluated appropriately. Too often suicide prevention programs do not use evidence-based research or practice methodologies. More funding is warranted to continue evidence-based studies in suicide. In accord with the United States Surgeon General, we support the position that the public should view mental illness or substance abuse disorders as a real illness. Public awareness could close the gap in the perception of mental illness and physical illness as two distinct separate issues. Increased public awareness regarding the frequency, treatment, and recovery process of mental illness, and the human rights of people with mental illness could reduce barriers to treatment and care. Suicidal persons with underlying mental illness who are seeking mental health treatment should be viewed as persons who are pursuing basic health care. Concomitantly, the United States Surgeon General reports that our nation is facing a public health crisis in pediatric mental health. This is of importance for pediatric populations because untreated mental illness is a known risk factor for youth suicide. According to the World Health Organization, countries have the responsibility to give priority to mental health in their health planning, as enlightened mental health policy, legislation, professional training, and sustainable fiscal resources will facilitate the delivery of the appropriate mental health services to those who need them at all levels of health care.

2

Culture-Specific Methods Are Needed to Prevent Teen Suicide

David B. Goldston et al.

David B. Goldston is affiliated with the Department of Psychiatry and Behavioral Sciences at the Duke University School of Medicine.

Adolescent suicide is widely recognized as a serious problem with serious consequences. Suicide prevention and intervention programs are increasingly available to assist suicidal youth. Yet, the significance of culture, race, and ethnicity to both adolescent suicide risk and adolescent suicide treatment remains overlooked. Consequently, the very populations that could benefit most from social and medical support in dealing with hopelessness and depression are unlikely to have their needs met.

Suicide is the third leading cause of death among adolescents, accounting for a greater number of deaths than the next seven leading causes of death combined for 15- to 24-year-olds. Almost 1 in 12 adolescents in high school made a suicide attempt, and 17% of adolescents seriously considered making a suicide attempt, in the calendar year 2005. Nonetheless, there are differences among ethnic groups in the rates and contexts within which adolescent suicidal behaviors occur.

David B. Goldston, Sherry Davis Molock, Leslie B. Whitbeck, Jessica L. Murakami, Luis H. Zaya, and Cordon C. Nagayama Hall, "Cultural Considerations in Adolescent Suicide Prevention and Psychosocial Treatment," *American Psychologist*, vol. 63, 2008, pp. 14,15, 17–25. Copyright © 2008 by the American Psychological Association. Reproduced with permission of the American Psychological Association, conveyed through Copyright Clearance Center, Inc.

The purpose of this article is to examine these ethnic differences and to explore the implications of culture for the development of suicide prevention and treatment interventions. . . .

As defined here, ethnic group differences can be considered to be a subset of cultural differences. There is a great deal of heterogeneity within ethnic groups, and differences due to ethnicity and culture may not be static insofar as culture is learned and may change over time. In addition, in our multiethnic society, it is common for families to comprise individuals from multiple ethnic backgrounds or heritage.

Suicidal behavior is a generic term in this article referring to thoughts of suicide, suicide attempts, and deaths by suicide. *Suicide* refers to a self-inflicted death associated with some (intrinsic or extrinsic) evidence of intent to kill oneself. *Suicide attempts* likewise refer to potentially self-injurious but non-lethal behavior associated with any intent to kill oneself. *Suicide ideation* refers to thoughts of killing oneself (regardless of intent).

Differences in Suicide Rates

Evidence of racial and ethnic differences is readily apparent in the rates of lethal and nonlethal suicidal behaviors among different groups of adolescents. . . . The rate of suicide deaths among adolescents differs by a factor of 20 between the highest risk group (American Indian/Alaska Native males) and the lowest risk group (African American females). . . . There is also a great deal of variability in rates of nonlethal suicide attempts. Specifically, suicide attempts are highest among American Indian/Alaska Native (AI/AN) females, followed by Latinas, AI/AN males, and Asian American/Pacific Islander (AA/PI) females; suicide attempts are lowest among African American and White adolescent males. Hand in hand with these differences in rates are differences in the precipitants associated with suicidal behavior, differences in risk and protective factors, and differences among groups in how they react to suicidal behavior and in how this reaction translates into help-seeking behaviors.

African American Youth

Although the overall suicide rate among African Americans aged 10–19 years declined from 4.5 to 3.0 per 100,000 in the United States from 1995 to 2004, suicide remains the third leading cause of death for African American 15- to 19-year-olds. From 1981 to 1995, the suicide rates increased 133% for 10- to 19-year-old African American youths; this increase was primarily evident among males. The increased rate over time of suicide deaths among young African American males was largely accounted for by an increase in rates of suicide deaths via firearms. Across the life span, the median age of suicide is approximately a decade earlier for Black suicide victims than for other suicide victims. Moreover, the rate of suicide attempts for African American adolescent males more than doubled from 1991 to 2001.

There appear to be no published studies of effective suicide prevention programs or treatments specifically tailored for African American youths.

There is much heterogeneity in the Black population that may affect risk for suicidal behaviors, including rural versus urban differences, regional differences, and differences between recent immigrants and individuals whose ancestors were brought to this country from Africa as slaves. Little has been written about cultural differences among Black youths and how they might be related to differential risk for suicidal behavior. However, in the National Survey of American Life, [S.] Joe, [R.] Baser, [G.] Breeden, [H.] Neighbors, and [J.] Jackson found that Black men of Caribbean descent in this country had higher rates of suicide attempts than African

American men and that Black adults in the southern United States had lower rates of suicide attempts than Black adults in other regions.

Cultural Context

Two widely prevalent stressors that have been linked to a number of physiological and psychological problems for African Americans are racism and discrimination. [R.] Clark and colleagues defined racism as "beliefs, attitudes, institutional arrangements, and acts that tend to denigrate individuals or groups because of phenotypic characteristics or ethnic group affiliation". Although not unique to African Americans, perceived racism and discrimination have been found to be associated with depression, increased substance use, and hopelessness among African American youths. These factors, in turn, are associated with adolescent suicidal behaviors.

Using city-level analyses, [C.] Kubrin, [T.] Wadsworth, and [S.] DiPietro demonstrated that deindustrialization in urban areas (inner cities) has been related to increased rates of suicide among 15- to 34-year-old African American males. Deindustrialization in the inner cities is related to a number of economic and social disadvantages, including greater concentrations of poverty; fewer opportunities for education, employment, and social mobility; a sense of hopelessness and alienation; greater violence; and fewer family and community social supports that might protect against suicidality. [M.] Greenberg and [D.] Schneider similarly argued that suicide and homicide rates are the highest for the urban poor because they live in impoverished areas with fewer resources and greater exposure to violence and toxic waste. Many African Americans attribute poor environmental conditions and limited opportunities to ethnic discrimination.

[J.] Gibbs described the importance of social support, cultural cohesion, and the role of extended family as factors that mitigate the risk of suicidal behaviors among African Americans. It has been hypothesized that African American females' greater access to familial and community protective mechanisms accounts in part for their lower rates of death by suicide. This underscores the ethos of communalism among some African Americans that emphasizes the extended self, social bonds, and the fundamental interdependence of people. However, on the basis of survey findings with young adult college students, [T.] Harris and [S.] Molock found that collectivist values may not always be protective and in fact may be related to higher rates of suicidal thoughts and depressive symptoms. It was suggested that individuals who are higher in a collectivist orientation may be more sensitized to the presence of racial oppression and discrimination that occurs in the college community and the community at large.

Prevention and Treatment

To date, there appear to be no published studies of effective suicide prevention programs or treatments specifically tailored for African American youths. Prevention programs developed for African American youths for reducing other public health problems have included a focus on increasing ethnic identity through rites of passage programs while simultaneously teaching African American youths new problem-solving skills.

[S.] Molock has suggested that the *Black Church* should be considered when developing suicide interventions because of the importance of religion and spirituality in African American culture. Although there are many different faith traditions within the African American community, a common religious/ cultural ethos underlies many African American Christian churches, collectively referred to as the *Black Church*. Although there has been some decline in its influence, the Black Church continues to have an influence on the African American community by providing social support and promoting self-reliance and political activism. In a series of qualitative studies, Molock and her colleagues found that African American church members and clergy were interested in developing mental health interventions in churches that would strengthen families and youths and were more likely to view suicide as aberrant to African American cultural values rather than as anathema to [rejected by] religious beliefs.

Nonetheless, potential barriers to consider within the Black Church include the fact that clergy are less likely to recognize suicidal lethality than other health professionals and make few referrals to mental health professionals and the fact that some Christian churches may have negative attitudes toward mental health treatment and suicide. It is possible that some of these barriers can be overcome through gatekeeper training programs for clergy and laypeople (i.e., training for individuals who have contact with youths so they are better able to recognize risk and make appropriate referrals).

American Indian populations have . . . earlier and higher rates of alcohol and drug use among youths.

American Indian and Alaska Natives

Suicide accounts for nearly one in five deaths among AI/AN 15- to 19-year-olds, a considerably higher proportion of deaths than for other ethnic groups. Differences in suicide rates between AI/AN youths and other ethnic youths have been noted for over three decades. As a consequence, by the 1970s, there were cautions to researchers and practitioners to avoid stereotypes of the "suicidal Indian." Gender differences in suicide deaths among AI/AN youths are somewhat attenuated relative to other ethnic groups because of the relatively higher rate of suicide among AI/AN females in recent years, a rate that is three times that of 15- to 19-year-old females in the general population.

The Cultural Context

AI/AN adolescents experience many of the same risk factors as other youths. Although two thirds of American Indian children live in urban areas, research over the last three decades has focused almost entirely on those who live on reservations. Life on rural, sometimes isolated reservations appears to amplify risks. For example, geographically isolated reservations may increase the likelihood of economic deprivation, lack of education, and limited employment opportunities, thereby contributing to a sense of hopelessness among young people.

Among the risk factors, American Indian populations have elevated rates of alcohol abuse and dependence disorder and earlier and higher rates of alcohol and drug use among youths, relative to most other ethnic groups, although this varies by culture and within culture. For example, according to data collected as part of the Monitoring the Future national survey from 1976 to 2000, almost a quarter of American Indian eighth graders reported drinking five or more drinks at a single sitting within the past two weeks. This rate of heavy drinking in eighth grade is higher than that reported for other ethnic groups, with the exception of Mexican American youths, who have a comparable rate. More severe or progressed alcohol and substance use, in turn, is more strongly associated with increased risk of suicidality. High rates of adult alcohol use in some communities may also weaken support systems for at-risk youths.

The military campaigns against and the forced relocation of American Indians have been well documented. In addition, during the late 1800s and throughout the first half of this century, AI/AN children were removed from their families and raised in boarding schools where traditional language use and cultural ways were forbidden. For those living on the reservations, the practice of traditional religions was illegal, and often there were few or no means of supporting a family, which created dependence on inadequate food distribution by the government. The sense of intergenerational trauma associated with this ethnic cleansing persists today, with daily reminders including reservation living and losses of traditional ways. This intergenerational trauma is associated with demoralization and hopelessness and may be associated with increased suicide risk.

The rate of suicide among [Asian American/Pacific Islander] males is the lowest for males among the ethnic groups.

Prevention and Treatment

Because they acknowledge tremendous diversity between the more than 562 federally recognized tribes of the United States and Canada, suicide prevention programs that are culturally appropriate and incorporate culturally specific knowledge and traditions have been shown to be well received by AI/AN communities and to have promising results. In one review, [D.] Middlebrook, [P.] LeMaster, [J.] Beals, [D.] Novins, and [S.] Manson identified nine prevention programs that met Institute of Medicine criteria for evaluating preventive interventions. Of these, five targeted AI/AN suicide among youths: the Zuni Life-Skills Development Curriculum, the Wind River Behavioral Program, the Tohono O'odham Psychology Service, the Western Athabaskan Natural Helpers Program, and the Indian Suicide Prevention Center. Four other AI/AN programs included suicide prevention as part of more general adolescent behavioral health programs. These prevention programs incorporate positive messages regarding cultural heritage that increase the self-esteem and sense of mastery among AI/AN adolescents and focus on protective factors in a culturally appropriate context. They also teach coping methods such as traditional ways of seeking social support.

The results of prevention efforts are promising. For example, the most recent follow-up report from the Western Athabaskan Natural Helpers Program indicated a decrease of 61% in suicide attempts during the 12 years the program has been implemented. [P.] May and colleagues attributed the success of this program to a comprehensive prevention strategy that addressed multiple levels of behavioral health problems, strong community investment in the program, and ongoing evaluation to maintain program focus.

Asian American and Pacific Islanders

AA/PIs are proportionally the fastest-growing ethnic group in the country, with estimates indicating that the number of AA/PI youths will increase by 74% by 2015. . . . The rate of suicide among AA/PI males is the lowest for males among the ethnic groups, and the gender differences in rates of suicide for AA/PI adolescents are not as large as those for other ethnic groups. However, AA/PIs are an extremely heterogeneous group with significant intergroup differences in rates of suicide. For example, suicide has been ranked as the leading cause of death among South Asians aged 15–24 in the United States. Nonetheless, as described below, suicide and suicidal behavior likely are underrecognized among AA/PI youths owing to a variety of factors.

The Cultural Context

When an individual's behavior upsets group harmony, loss of face (social shame) is experienced. Loss of face is more prominent in East Asians (i.e., Chinese and Japanese) and East Asian Americans, although it may also exist in other Asian groups (e.g., South Asians) to a lesser degree, and it persists despite acculturation. Loss of face can serve as a precipitant for suicidal behavior if the loss of face is perceived as intolerable or if the group views suicide as an honorable way of dealing with difficulties. Alternatively, if the group views suicide as dishonorable, the adolescent may be less likely to attempt suicide, even in the presence of loss of face.

There is a tendency among many AA/PIs to value interdependence, that is, a collectivist orientation, over independence. Whereas independence promotes individuality and competitiveness and places a high value on personal standards, among individuals of Asian descent, a collectivist orientation may be associated with conformity, clearly defined roles, and the importance of group harmony. This association may result in the use of indirect communication, suppression of conflict, and the withholding of free expression of feelings. Indeed, AA/PI adolescents report greater difficulty discussing problems with their family members and are often less emotionally expressive than their non-Asian peers. Together with fear of loss of face, this emphasis on interdependence may contribute to the concealment of emotional disturbance in AA/PI adolescents and to a possible lack of awareness by others of suicide risk.

We found no programs for prevention of suicide among [Asian American/Pacific Islander] youths.

AA/PI adolescents may experience distress and conflict with family members and peers when there are conflicts between the demands of role fulfillment and interdependence and the demands for establishment of an independent identity, as valued in Western society. In a study by [M.] Lorenzo, [A.] Frost, and [H.] Reinherz, for example, older Asian American adolescents reported more social problems than their peers, including peer rejection, teasing, and being too dependent on others. Such strains may increase vulnerability to depression and suicidality.

The level of acculturation [the process by which values and behaviors are acquired] and recency of immigration may influence suicidal behavior in AA/PI adolescents. The immigration process itself may present significant stresses for some

AA/PI individuals, particularly refugees who have endured trauma, violence, and life-threatening conditions and journeys. Most of the research documenting stresses among Asian refugees has focused on adults, but [I.] Hyman, [N.] Vu, and [M.] Beiser noted multiple acculturative stresses experienced by children of Southeast Asian refugees, including feelings of estrangement and academic frustrations related to lack of English fluency, unequal language fluency between parents and youths, cultural differences in academic environments, and high parental expectations.

Prevention and Treatment

The prevention literature for AA/PI youths is sparse. In geographical areas with larger concentrations of AA/PIs, community-driven efforts focused on the prevention of problems such as violence have been described. Such prevention efforts often include programs such as case management, education, and crisis intervention, but the majority of these efforts have not been evaluated. We found no programs for prevention of suicide among AI/PI youths.

Expectations of obligation to the family appear to play an important role in Latina suicidal behaviors.

Inclusion of family members may facilitate assessment and treatment for suicidality. Because AA/PI cultures value interdependence, it is not surprising that Asian Americans receiving mental health treatment tend to have persistent and intensive family member involvement. [K.] Lin and [F.] Cheung, for example, caution that clinicians unfamiliar with Asian culture may view family members' insistence on being involved with treatment as inappropriate or pathological and may run the risk of humiliating clients and their family members through confrontation of this behavior.

Suicidality Among Latinos

Latino youths may be less likely than some other groups to die by suicide, but Latinas in particular report relatively high rates of hopelessness, suicide plans, and suicide attempts in the past year. Most lifetime suicide attempts described by Latinos in the National Latino and Asian American Study (NLAAS) occurred when they were younger than 18 years of age. U.S.-born Latino adolescents are more likely to attempt suicide than are foreign-born Latino youths. Adolescent Latinas are consistently twice as likely as Latino males (15% to 8%) to report suicide attempts during the preceding 12 months. Although Latinos in the United States are a heterogeneous Hispanic population, intergroup differences among adolescents have not been well studied. There are common cultural factors, however, that span Latino groups and that can help explain the higher rates of suicide attempts among Latino youths.

The Cultural Context

Expectations of obligation to the family appear to play an important role in Latina suicidal behaviors. In spite of the fact that family closeness and good relations with parents have been found to be a resiliency factor for suicidality among Latino males and females. In Latino cultures, individuals typically are socialized to be oriented toward the centrality of family in their lives, to identify with the family, and to place obligation to family over obligation to the self or outsiders. This orientation, known as *familism*, influences the sense of individual identity, placing a premium on family unity and cooperation as well as reverence to parents and family elders. The emphasis on collective goals, rather than individualism, among some Latinos, is similar to the emphasis on interdependence in many Asian American cultures.

Adolescents may experience stress because of the conflicting messages that they receive at home and in the majority culture about independence, responsibility to the family, child-rearing practices, and parent-adolescent relations. For example, Latino families may emphasize the demure, controlled, nurturing behavior known as *marianismo* for their daughters while fostering a behavioral style among their sons that emphasizes being assertive and a family protector, commonly known as *machismo*. The more dependent, family-centered *marianismo* may place Latinas at odds with families as needs for peer involvement and approval and strivings for autonomy become prominent in adolescence. Familism is especially evident in recently immigrated Latinos and appears to endure in subsequent generations.

Engagement of families of suicidal youths is important in any culture, but particularly so for many Latinos.

Other factors that influence suicidal behavior are the impact of the often traumatic immigration process and acculturation. For example, some youths endure life-threatening circumstances and are forced to leave some family members behind when they emigrate. . . . Nonetheless, immigrant youths are more likely than their parents to adopt the values, beliefs, and behaviors associated with the new culture, and differential rates of acculturation can create tension in Latino families. Such discrepancies may increase the level of conflicts between parents and adolescents, resulting in dysfunctional outcomes such as suicide attempts and psychological maladjustment.

Prevention and Treatment

There are, to our knowledge, no published, empirically based suicide prevention or treatment interventions developed exclusively for Latinos. However, there have been adaptations of other therapies for other disorders (e.g., depression, substance abuse) that are informative. For example, in recognition of the cultural value of *familism*, [J.] Rosselló and [G.] Bernal adapted cognitive-behavioral and interpersonal therapies for depressed Puerto Rican adolescents so that the intervention involved parents in the treatment of their adolescent. This approach was consistent with the expectations of Latino adolescents regarding the inclusion of their parents and provided opportunities for parents to better understand their adolescent's socioemotional needs within the perspective of their cultural expectations and the context in which their child was developing.

Engagement of families of suicidal youths is important in any culture, but particularly so for many Latinos, given views about the centrality of family. In this regard, a cost-effective means of engaging parents of Latino adolescent suicide attempters has been reported that includes the use of videotapes to modify treatment expectations and training programs for staff to enhance their sensitivity to Latino parents' reactions to the suicide attempts and to the service process. In addition, the efficacy of strategic structural systems engagement (SSSE), an approach for bringing hard-to-reach families into treatment, also has been shown with Latino families. For example, in a study conducted in Miami of youth at risk for drug abuse, SSSE improved overall engagement in therapy. Close analyses revealed that the results differed depending on the Latino group studied. Specifically, non-Cuban Latino families responded extremely well to the intervention, but families of Cuban origin did not. The authors speculated that the Cuban Latinos differed from other Latinos in several key respects, including their levels of acculturation, individualism, and orientation to the values of the mainstream culture. As these findings on SSSE show, differences among Latino groups exist and must be considered in prevention efforts and treatment of suicidal Latino youths and their families.

3

Bullying Increases Teen Suicide Risk

Karen Dineen Wagner

Karen Dineen Wagner is the Marie B. Gale Centennial Professor and vice chair of the Department of Psychiatry and Behavioral Sciences.

According to a study published in the Journal of the American Academy of Child and Adolescent Psychiatry *in 2007, both adolescents who fall victim to bullying behavior and adolescents who engage in bullying behavior are at increased risk for suicidal thinking. Approximately 20 percent of study participants reported that they had been bullied in school and 25 percent of study participants reported that they had bullied others in school. This study reveals the drastic effects of a fairly common occurrence. But it does not account for the increasingly widespread phenomenon of online bullying. Recognizing that bullying goes on in cyber communities only further underscores the real outcomes of adolescent bullying, including suicide.*

In 2007, an important study was published that examined bullying and its potential association with depression and suicidal behavior in adolescents. A unique feature of this study was that it assessed bullying behavior and suicide attempts in victims of bullying, persons who exhibited bullying behavior, and bully-victims (adolescents who were bullies and victims of bullying). In addition, the study examined bullying behavior both in and out of school settings.

Adolescents aged 13 to 19 years who were enrolled in grades 9 through 12 in suburban schools in New York were included. A total of 2341 students who attended school from fall 2002 to spring 2004 completed a questionnaire; the sample was predominantly white (80%) and 58% were male. The questions related to the 4 weeks before the study, although the reporting period for suicide attempts was lifetime. Researchers used the Beck Depression Inventory to assess depression and the Suicide Ideation Questionnaire to asess suicidal ideation [thoughts of suicide without acting out]. Suicide attempt history included any attempt, regardless of extent of injury. With regard to bullying behavior, students were asked how often they had been bullied or had bullied others in and out of school during the past 4 weeks. "Being bullied" was defined as having student(s) say or do unpleasant things or being teased repeatedly in a way the person does not like.

The risk of depression, suicidal ideation, and suicide attempt was significantly higher for students who were considered either a victim or a bully compared with students who were not.

Teen Bullying Is Widespread

About 20% of students reported that they were victims of bullying in school and about 10% reported that they were victims of bullying outside school. With regard to bullying behavior, about 25% of students reported that they bullied other students in school and 15% reported that they bullied others outside school.

These percentages of bullying behaviors are quite high, particularly since the time frame for reporting these events was only 4 weeks. Boys were more likely than girls to be victims of bullying in school, whereas boys and girls were equally likely to be victims of bullying outside school.

The risk of depression, suicidal ideation, and suicide attempt was significantly higher for students who were considered either a victim or a bully compare with students who were not. This association was noted whether bullying behavior occurred in or out of school. The more frequent the bullying behavior (either as a victim or bully), the greater the risk of depression, suicidal ideation, or suicide attempt.

For example, adolescents who were frequent victims of bullying in school were 5 times as likely to have serious suicidal ideation and 4 times as likely to attempt suicide as students who had not been victims. Similarly, students who frequently bullied others in school were 3 times as likely to have serious suicidal ideation and suicide attempts as those who did not bully others in school and were 5 times as likely to have serious suicidal ideation and suicide attempts as those who did not bully others outside of school. Even when bullying was infrequent (less than weekly), the likelihood of suicidal behavior was about 2 times greater in both victims and bullies in and out of school than in those who were not bullied. Students who were considered to be bully-victims frequently were at the highest risk for depression and suicidal behavior.

Clinicians should inquire about bullying when evaluating and treating teenagers, especially those who have depression.

The authors of the study concluded that bullying might be a marker of suicidal behavior. They recommended that prevention of bullying should be part of suicide prevention efforts. A relevant component of this study was that it examined bullying behavior outside the school setting. Although bullying behavior (as the victim or bully) was found to be more common in school than it was outside school, it is important to note that this study was conducted from 2002 to 2004.

With the burgeoning use of cyberspace, it would be interesting to learn whether the frequency of reported bullying outside school has increased.

Cyber-bullying

In 2001, I wrote a column "Too Much Bullying in Our Schools"; since then, the Internet and cell phones have, unfortunately, provided increased opportunities for bullying outside school that do not require face-to-face confrontation. Recent news has focused on the rise of cyber-bullying. For example, in a Google search of bullying and cyberspace in January 2007, there were 278,000 citations. Whereas bullying in school is restricted to students in that school, the Internet provides access to nearly limitless numbers of people. Many teenagers are adept at text messaging on cell phones, creating Web sites and blogs, instant messaging, and creating videos that can be transmitted instantly. Poignant stories have been written about teenagers who were victims of cyber-bullying and felt that aspects of their lives were ruined by this experience.

Addressing Bullying and Suicide

The seriousness of bullying, particularly as it relates to suicidal behavior, is exemplified in the findings from the study described. It is important for clinicians to be aware of the high prevalence of bullying behavior (either as victim, bully, or both) in adolescents. Moreover, students who are bullied in school may not be able to escape the bullying when they are at home because of current communications technology. Clinicians should inquire about bullying when evaluating and treating teenagers, especially those who have depression. Similarly, clinicians should inform parents about the serious clinical implications of bullying and recommend that they talk with their teenager about the bullying behavior that may be occurring both in and outside school.

4

Substance Use Increases Teen Suicide Risk

Michael S. Dunn, Bruce Goodrow, Connie Givens, and Susan Austin

Michael S. Dunn is an associate professor in the Department of Public Health at East Tennessee State University. Bruce Goodrow is the research and development coordinator for Tennessee's Rural Health Service Consortium. Connie Givens is the executive director of Coordinated School Health for the Tennessee Department of Education. Susan Austin is the evaluation coordinator for the Department of Public Health at East Tennessee State University.

While many studies have shown that high schoolers who engage in illegal substance use are at increased risk for considering and attempting suicide, few studies have drawn links between substance use and suicidality among middle schoolers. As results from the 2004 Youth Risk Behavior Survey indicated, however, rural adolescents in middle school who use illegal substances face increased likelihood of engaging in suicidal behavior. Thus, suicide prevention programs that address even the youngest of adolescents must take substance use into consideration.

Adolescent suicide is a serious public health issue that has yet to be dealt with in an effective manner. Suicide is the third leading cause of death for adolescents and young adults in the United States. It has been estimated that nearly 3 mil-

Michael S. Dunn, Bruce Goodrow, Connie Givens, and Susan Austin, "Substance Use Behavior and Suicide Indicators Among Rural Middle School Students," *Journal of School Health*, vol. 78, January, 2008. Reproduced with permission of Blackwell Publishing Ltd.

lion adolescents, between the ages of 12 and 17 years, contemplate suicide each year, of which almost 37% attempt suicide. Given the tremendous impact suicide has on society, it is important to identify factors that predispose people to take one's own life to prevent suicide from occurring in school age youth.

The Impact of Alcohol and Drug Use

Substance use and abuse is a risk factor for suicide. Studies have consistently demonstrated that suicide attempts are more likely to occur among adolescents who abuse alcohol and/or use illicit drugs. Research has found that problematic adolescent drinkers tend to have higher suicidal ideation [thoughts of suicide] prevalence rates and suicide attempts compared with non-adolescent and moderate adolescent drinkers. Alcohol and other drug use may impair judgment, and alcohol intoxication is often found among adolescents who have attempted suicide. Studies have found a consistent positive correlation between adolescent drinking and suicide ideation and behavior. Moreover, it has been suggested that long-term use or abuse of alcohol and other drugs may damage social relationship and social support, which in turn may increase the likelihood of suicidal thoughts and behaviors, as substance use has been shown to impair emotional stability and cognitive rationale. Substance use may cause emotional instability and cognitive disturbances, thereby producing feelings and thoughts in people that may not be rational.

Most studies to date have focused on high school students with established patterns of substance use and abuse. Studies focusing on suicidal ideation and behavior and substance use in middle school students in a rural state have been lacking. As such, the purpose of this study was to provide a descriptive profile of substance use behaviors and the prevalence of suicide indicators (thought about, considered, and planned) among rural middle school students and to examine the association between substance use and suicidal indicators among middle school students completing the 2004 middle school Youth Risk Behavior Survey (YRBS). To our knowledge, this is the first study to date that has examined the relationship between substance use and suicidal behavior among rural middle school students.

How the Study Was Conducted

Subjects

Participants consisted of a convenience sample [a sample where the participants where selected at the convenience of the researcher] of 10,273 middle school students (sixth to eighth grade) attending 10 public schools in rural Tennessee. The schools were selected based on there participation in a Coordinated School Health pilot program in Tennessee. The 10 school systems represented diverse schools throughout Tennessee. Four school systems were located in west Tennessee, 3 school systems were located in middle Tennessee, and 3 school systems were located in east Tennessee. The median family income was $33,000 and the average population size was 39,000 of the 10 school system sites. All students in 10 selected school systems were eligible to participate.

Instrument

The middle school YRBS was used in this study and is designed to determine the various health-risk behaviors of middle school students. The questionnaire measured demographics, height and weight, unintentional injury, violence, suicide ideation and attempts, tobacco use, drug and alcohol use, sexual risk taking, weight control, and physical activity. Measures of unintentional injury, violence, suicide ideation and behavior, drug and alcohol use, and sexual risk taking were limited to lifetime use. Tobacco smoking was measured with variables of initiation, daily smoking, and past 30 days smoking. Smokeless tobacco and cigar use were measured with variables of initiation and past 30 days use.

Procedures

Data collection took place during April and May 2004. All data were collected on site at the participating schools. Prior to administering the questionnaire, a consent process was implemented by each school. Seven of 10 school systems opted for a passive consent process in which consent forms were sent home to parents, and parents were instructed to sign and return the form if they did not want their child to participate in the study. The other school systems opted for active consent in which consent forms were sent home for parents/ guardians to sign and return to the teacher administering the survey.

Several substance use variables were found to be predictive of planning to commit suicide.

Teachers were responsible for administering the survey to their students. All classes within each school system were surveyed during a particular time in the school day. Teachers were instructed how to administer the questionnaire by a protocol developed for this study. Upon completion, students returned their questionnaire to the teacher. Completed questionnaires were not viewed by anyone associated with the schools but were mailed directly to a third party (Research Triangle Institute) for scoring and compilation onto SPSS [Statistical Package for the Social Sciences] spreadsheets. Names were not recorded on the questionnaire to protect student identity. The response rate was estimated to be 93% and was based on the number of students who did not complete the survey due to either not having parental permission, refusing to participate on the day the survey was administered, or was absent from school on the day the survey was administered.

Data Analysis

Demographic information about respondents included race, age, gender, and educational level. Chi-square analysis [analysis used to determine differences between categories and compare observed results with expected results] was used to examine the variables related to differences between males and females in regard to suicide ideation and substance use behavior.

Questions related to suicidal ideation and behavior included the following: "Have you ever seriously thought about killing yourself?" "Have you ever made a plan about how to kill yourself?" "Have you ever tried to kill yourself?" and represent the dependent variables for the analysis.

Independent variables included substance use behavior questions. Cigarette use variables consisted of ever use, past 30 days use, and daily cigarette smoking behavior. Other tobacco use included past 30 days use of smokeless tobacco and cigars, cigarillos, or little cigars use. Alcohol and marijuana use variables consisted of ever use. Four questions measured other drug use behavior, including ever use of cocaine, inhalants, steroids, and intravenous (IV) drug use. . . .

Findings of the Study

Several substance use variables were found to be predictive of planning to commit suicide. Females who had planned to commit suicide were more likely than those who had not planned to commit suicide to have initiated smoking. Additionally, 69% of suicide planners had initiated alcohol use and were found to be 2.24 times more likely to use alcohol than those who had not planned the act. Also, it was found that 14.6% and 40.0% of suicide planners had initiated cocaine and inhalant use, respectively, and were 1.65 and 1.57 times more likely to have used those drugs than those who had not planned the act of suicide. Additional significant predictors of planning to commit suicide included steroid use and past 30 days smoking. Among males, 70.1% and 69.2% had initiated cigarette and alcohol use, respectively, and were found to be 1.65 and 1.57 times more likely to have used those drugs than those who had not planned to commit suicide. Additionally, it was found that 23.7% and 43.2% of planners had initiated cocaine and inhalant use.

Several substance use variables were found to be predictive of trying to commit suicide. Among females [those who engaged in] smoking, drinking, marijuana, cocaine, and inhalant initiation were more likely to have tried to commit suicide. Of those who had tried to commit suicide, more than 75% had initiated smoking, 72% had initiated drinking, and 41.9% had initiated marijuana use. Additionally, it was found that females who had tried to commit suicide, 18.6% had initiated cocaine use and 46% had initiated inhalant use when compared with females who had not tried to commit suicide. Among males, smoking (74.1%), cocaine (30.8%), inhalant initiation (48.8%), and daily smoking (39.6%) were highly associated with having tried to commit suicide.

It is important to identify and address the occurrences of substance use behaviors among students as this factor has been shown to increase the likelihood of suicidal ideation in adolescents.

Suicide Prevention and Substance Use

Limited research has been conducted with rural middle school students participating in the Coordinated School Health Program and the role of substance use on suicide ideation and behavior. This research shows the need to target substance use behaviors at an early age. This research with middle school students found that there were high rates of substance use behavior and suicidal thoughts/behavior and that there was a relationship between the two. Among the total sample, 23.4%

had thought about suicide, 15.9% had planned to commit suicide, and 10.0% had tried to commit suicide. This is higher than the national average of 20.1%, 13.3%, and 8.9% for thought about, planned, and tried to commit suicide, respectively.

Based on the findings from this study, it seems that suicide prevention programs should be designed, tested, and implemented during the early middle school grades. Moreover, such programs should focus on preventing tobacco, alcohol, marijuana, and other drug use behaviors. Also, findings from this study support the conclusions of other researchers who found that adolescents who engage in substance use were more likely to experience suicidal ideation and behavior than abstaining youth. It has been reported that suicide attempts are most common during mid-adolescent (13–17 years), which corresponds with the eighth grade. Therefore, the middle school years are the ideal time to identify factors that may contribute to suicidal behavior. As this research has found, a large percentage of middle school students had initiated the use of various substances were at increased risk for suicidal thoughts and behaviors.

Adolescent suicide is a significant issue in the United States that has yet to be dealt with in an effective manner. High rates of suicidal behavior still prevail in the United States and trends have shown little changes. According to the Centers for Disease Control and Prevention, during the past 10 years [1998–2008], there have been no significant changes in adolescent suicide attempts. The school setting provides a great opportunity to assist with adolescent suicide prevention. To prevent the occurrence of suicide among adolescents, it is important to identify and address the occurrences of substance use behaviors among students as this factor has been shown to increase the likelihood of suicidal ideation in adolescents. Individuals that make up the coordinated school health team need to take a proactive stance toward this issue and to develop and implement policies and programs for the prevention of suicide among youths, especially in reducing the factors that contribute to the behavior such as alcohol, tobacco, and other drug use behavior. School personnel need to be aware of these relationships since they serve in potential gate keeper roles in identifying problem behaviors and referring students to appropriate care. At the present time, suicide prevention programs in school settings often target the gatekeepers and provide training to them on identifying the major risk factors for adolescent suicide (ie, substance use).

Limitations of Study

The findings of this study must be considered in light of several limitations. First, the sample was one of convenience. Thus, the generalization of the findings must be done with caution. Second, the survey was self-report behavior, which may have resulted in some response bias by the students. There is no way to ensure the accuracy of the responses. However, steps were taken to ensure the reliability of the measures by assuring the subjects that the questionnaire was completely anonymous and by requesting honest responses. Third, the students were from a rural setting, limiting the generalizability of the findings.

5

Self-Harm May Be Related to Teen Suicide Risk

CommunityCare

CommunityCare is a Web site dedicated to providing information on social work and social care issues.

Self-harm, which can involve a range of behaviors, including but not limited to drug overdosing and cutting, is most prevalent in adolescents over the age of sixteen. It is interpreted by mental health professionals as a physical manifestation of psychological pain that may lead to more serious suicide attempts. Some teens however, argue that while self-harm and suicide are connected, self-harm can actually serve as a suicide prevention technique.

Overdose and cutting are the two most common forms of self-harm reported for children and young people. Self-harm becomes more common after the age of 16, but is still prevalent among younger children. Self-harm may indicate a temporary period of emotional pain or distress, or deeper mental health issues, which may result in suicide. A great deal of the research and policy literature on the subject does not distinguish between self-harm with the intention of committing suicide and self-harm without that intention (sometimes called self-injury or self-mutilation). In this article, self-harm is used to include both types of behaviour.

Girls have been found to be much more likely to self-harm than boys. This means that much of the research into risk factors for self-harming has focused on girls and may not always reflect why boys self-harm. However, some factors that affect boys more than girls have been identified. These include problems concerning studying, money and housing.

Parents can be unaware that their children are self-harming. It is usually a private act and many children and young people who self-harm may not seek medical assistance or approach medical services. If the young person does not seek help or present at A&E [accident and emergency] departments with clear indications it can be difficult to recognise self-harm. However, one study of attempted suicide cases among 15-year-olds found that they were twice as likely to go to their GP [general practice doctor] than 15-year-olds who did not attempt suicide. They were also much more likely to present to their GP with mental health concerns or upper respiratory tract infection, for which there were no physical symptoms.

Self-Harm Triggers

Self-harm episodes can be triggered by either specific events or more general feelings of distress. Children aged five to 10 were more likely to self-harm if they had experienced stressful life events, such as witnessing domestic violence, having a family break-up, being placed in care, their parents or carers had an unwanted pregnancy or bereavement. Child abuse, both physical and sexual, has been found by several studies to be an important factor in the self-harming of some young people.

Children and adolescents are also much more likely to harm themselves if they are around other people who self-harm. Self-harm by friends or family has been found to trigger self-harm among adolescents. Self-harm behaviour can also have a group dynamic. Young people may get into self-harming groups at school, college or elsewhere and it may also form part of "rituals of initiation". Research shows that many children and young people who self-harm are also experiencing problems at school, such as work or exam pressures, but bullying is the most common issue.

Among five- to 15-year-olds, self-harm has been found to be about twice as prevalent among children from the lowest socio-economic income group and those living in rented accommodation. Socio-economic adversity or deprivation has also been found to be a significant independent factor associated with self-harm among adolescents and young people.

Link to Adolescent Suicide

When asked why they self-harm, children and young people put forward many reasons. They may have issues with self-esteem or they may feel frustrated and angry. Many say they cut or burn themselves, or perform other forms of self-harm, because it is a form of escapism, a release or relief from the pressure of mental, emotional or personal problems. Self-harm may provide a physical release from unbearable emotional or mental pressures. Some see it as a strategy to protect themselves, an effective means of coping. It makes the unmanageable manageable. Some describe it as suicide prevention strategy because it provides enough temporary relief from a range of pressures for which suicide may be thought to be the only release. However, some young people also say that self injury can be performed as a punishment, something that is "deserved", either for something that has happened in the past or something that is happening in the present.

Difficulties Addressing Self-Harm

Young people have also said that self-harming can "feel good" and that they do not feel that they should stop as the action performs an important and worthwhile function for them and does not harm anyone. Professionals may therefore face a difficult challenge with young people who self-harm because they may feel a responsibility to protect children from harming themselves, but their intervention may be neither wanted nor reduce the self-injurious behaviour.

Latina Teens Face Increased Suicide Risk

Laura Sessions Stepp

Laura Sessions Stepp is a Washington Post *staff writer.*

Adolescent Latinas constitute a large and growing minority group in the United States. Thus, the fact that young Latinas contemplate and attempt suicide at a disproportionately high rate should be of great social concern. Caught between cultures and attending schools that might not embrace cultural diversity, Latinas often face isolation and depression. While strong maternal figures can help deter young Latinas from suicidal thoughts and behaviors, larger community institutions must become more aware of the struggles that young Latinas face.

The second time Michelle, 16, swallowed sleeping pills, she collapsed on the living room floor. It was late at night, and her mom, Maribel, jumped up from her chair, managed to pick up her skinny, 5-foot-10-inch eldest daughter, slapped her a couple of times hoping to bring her back to consciousness, and let go. Michelle fell down again and her eyes rolled back. Maribel, who's from Puerto Rico, says she thought Michelle was drunk. She grabbed a blanket and a pillow and lay down next to Michelle, thinking her daughter would eventually wake up. A few hours later, the sun rose over their small home in a working-class section of New York City and, unable to rouse Michelle, Maribel yelled at someone in the house to call 911. An ambulance arrived along with a couple of police officers, one of whom suggested Michelle was faking unconsciousness. "You're daughter's probably just joking," he told her.

Suicide attempts can spread like a virus, from girlfriend to girlfriend.

It was no joke. Michelle had swallowed an entire bottle of Ambien [a sleep aid] and didn't wake until she had been checked into a nearby hospital in the Bronx. She spent two days there. She then was transferred to a psychiatric unit in Manhattan—one young Latina among approximately 2 million in the United States who have attempted suicide.

More Likely to Try Suicide

Latinas ages 12 to 17 are the largest minority group of girls in the country, and growing. They are more likely to try to take their lives than any other racial or ethnic group their age. Twenty-five percent say they've thought about suicide, according to the Centers for Disease Control and Prevention, and about 15 percent attempt it, compared with approximately 10 percent of white and black teen girls. Other studies put the proportion of attempters at 20 percent—slightly less than the fraction who smoke cigarettes.

In most cases, a girl swallows pills at home, according to Luis Zayas, a psychologist and professor of social work at Washington University in St. Louis. Zayas is in the middle of a five-year study of more than 150 young Latina girls who have attempted suicide. He says cutting is also finding a following among Latinas. The physical pain of cutting helps to mask their emotional pain, says Carolina Hausman, a social worker who assists Zayas. "These adolescents have intense emotions and no tools to process them," she adds. "Their body has to be calmed down somehow. They talk about seeing blood go down their wrist as a release."

Suicide attempts can spread like a virus, from girlfriend to girlfriend. Michelle—whose last name, like some others in this article, has been withheld to protect her privacy—says she knew of two girls who had made attempts before she did. A friend of one girl Hausman works with not only told the girl how to cut herself but advised her to minimize the pain by putting Vaseline on the area. Zayas and other experts suggest that suicide attempts like these are more a cry for help than evidence of a will to die. Were these girls living in the countries they or their parents were born in—where they might enjoy strong ties to relatives, communities and familiar customs—there's a good chance they wouldn't feel a need to act out, Zayas says. But here they struggle with feelings of powerlessness and frustration, torn between an American popular culture that encourages them to be sexy and assertive, and family expectations that they be modest and submissive. Add to that the isolation they may feel in school and you get some pretty depressed teenagers, Zayas says. They rarely seek help, partly because they and their parents are suspicious of mental health services and believe in keeping family troubles in the family. "Crossing the border," Zayas says, "can be hazardous to Latinas' health. Until we understand the cultural conflict, we will not be able to prevent this."

Jocelyn's case

Jocelyn Garay's parents, who fled the war in El Salvador in the early 1980s, always demanded a lot of their bubbly, dark-haired daughter: that she excel in school, help out with housework, be attentive to her younger sister and attend church. Her father, who, true to Hispanic custom, considered himself the boss of the family, had a hard time understanding why she wanted to do anything else. He considered some common teen social activities to be unnecessary, even dangerous. She says he forbade her from going to sleepovers at her friends' houses until she was 18. He said no when she asked to try out for the cheerleading team. He opposed dance lessons and put her in taekwondo instead, wanting her to learn to defend herself in what seemed to him (though not to his daughter, who was born here) a strange land.

Jocelyn, a high school senior in northern Virginia, says she has never tried to kill herself. But she has thought about it.

Washington psychologist Lillian Comas-Diaz, who counsels immigrants, says parents often don't understand that for many adolescents here, social success inspires motivation and academic success. What parents do know is that by moving to the United States they left behind the relatives, friends and neighbors who would have watched out for their daughter. They may be more rigid than they would have been back home—and meanwhile their daughter is hearing from her non-Latino friends, "Think about yourself and what you want. Forget your parents." The daughter, then, tries to be dutiful at home and to fit in at school, what Comas-Diaz calls being "of the divided heart."

The phrase describes Jocelyn in middle school and early high school. She spent much of that time being angry both at her father for having what she considered unrealistically high academic expectations and at herself for failing to meet them. She joined a Hispanic gang in seventh grade and alienated her white friends. In the spring of ninth grade, her father finally let go of his opposition to cheerleading and she made the team, only to be chastised by her Hispanic friends as being "whitewashed." "I don't want to live anymore," she remembers telling her younger sister. "If I'm not comfortable at home or school, what's the point?" "Don't do it," she recalls her sister saying. "Please, don't leave me alone."

Jocelyn never acted on her thoughts. Her mother has an intuitive sense of the pull between family and classmates, Jocelyn says, and helped her navigate her father's demands. [In 2007], Jocelyn joined a Girl Scout troop, where she found encouraging adults and new, upbeat friends. She now considers her father her biggest champion and her mom her closest friend. . . .

[Latinas'] schools and neighborhoods need preventive mental health services more attuned to Hispanic culture.

The Mother's Role

A Latina's relationship with her mother is the single biggest factor in whether that girl copes well with stress, according to a study published by Fordham University's Graduate School of Social Service. "It's not just being loved, but knowing they're loved," says Edgardo Menvielle, a psychiatrist at Washington's Children's Hospital who also works at the Cliniqua de Pueblo in Adams Morgan [neighborhood of D.C.] Zayas can spot the difference quickly by listening to a girl talk. "It's the difference between 'My mother doesn't understand' and 'My mother is old-fashioned but she listens.'"

Some Latina mothers—exhausted by fighting with boyfriends, raising children and working several jobs, or burdened by their own emotional problems—have trouble showing mother love. Paula, a petite high school senior with curly black hair and a big smile, says her mother used to be that way. The two of them immigrated to New York from Ecuador four years ago, in part to escape Paula's violent father. Paula's relationship with her mother was strained after their arrival, and she believed her aunt, whose home they moved into, resented her presence. Paula knew no English as she started high school. At home, she was expected to keep her aunt's house clean, wash the dishes and do the laundry. Overwhelmed early one evening that first year, she sought out a bottle of high-dose Motrin, a painkiller, and took one pill. This past September, it was two pills. She was looking at the bottle, wondering whether to take more, when a good friend called and she told him what she was doing. The friend came over, took her to the emergency room and stayed with her until her mom arrived.

Therapists see this pattern frequently: A girl chooses something a parent wouldn't notice—a pill or two, a light scratch with a sharp instrument. The next time it's two or three pills or a deeper cut, then more. With each attempt, the girl is more likely to die, which is why early intervention is critical.

More Assistance Needed

Social worker Hausman, herself a Latina, worries about girls like Paula who come from lower-income homes. She wonders about their mental health long-term, given the continuing conflict in their families and lack of outside resources. Their schools and neighborhoods need preventive mental health services more attuned to Hispanic culture, she says—starting with parenting classes. "In middle- and upper-class families, success is expected," she says. "If a child's mental health interferes with success, it tends to be noticed earlier. Low-income parents don't expect anything of their girls. Every middle-class mother tells me she wants her daughter to be a professional at 24, married with three children. These mothers want their girls to do the laundry."

Poor Body Image Increases Teen Suicide Risk

Amy M. Brausch and Jennifer J. Muehlenkamp

Amy M. Brausch completed her master's in psychology at Northern Illinois University. Jennifer J. Muehlenkamp is a faculty member in the Department of Psychology at the University of North Dakota.

Adolescence is widely recognized as a period of rapid physical and emotional change, as well as increased self-doubt and self-consciousness. Studies have repeatedly shown that teenagers are particularly susceptible to both poor body image and suicidal thoughts. Yet, the connection between poor body image and suicidal thinking has largely been overlooked. According to the responses of 231 male and female adolescents, however, this connection is an important one. When questioned about their past and present suicidal thoughts and their attitudes toward their bodies, these students revealed strong links between poor body image and suicidal tendencies.

Suicide is the third leading cause of death for 15 to 24-year-olds in the United States. Much of the research conducted on risk factors for suicide in adolescent samples has focused upon "traditional" risk factors such as depression, hopelessness, and past suicidal behavior. While valuable, these factors alone have been insufficient in their ability to fully account

Amy M. Brausch and Jennifer J. Muehlenkamp. "Body Image and Suicidal Ideation in Adolescents," *Body Image*, vol. 4, no. 2, 2007, pp. 207, 208, 211, 212. Copyright © 2007 Elsevier B.V. All rights reserved. Reprinted with permission from Elsevier, conveyed through Copyright Clearance Center, Inc.

for suicide risk in adolescents. Much of the existing research tends to omit other factors that are highly relevant to this age group, such as attitudes toward the body.

Poor body attitudes were related to suicidal ideation for both males and females.

Impact of Body Image

Adolescence is a time characterized by great emotional, social, and physical change, and as a result poor body image, depression, and eating disorders are among the most widespread disorders with an onset in adolescence. While females tend to experience greater discomfort and dissatisfaction with their changing bodies than do males, a negative body image is prevalent in up to 40% of males as well. This is concerning, given that self-esteem is largely influenced by body image in adolescents, and poor self-esteem is linked to suicide. Body dissatisfaction has consistently been identified as a risk factor for the development of depression and eating disorders both of which are associated with increased risk for suicide. Despite these documented relationships, very few studies have considered body image a unique risk factor for adolescent suicide.

[L.] Orbach proposed that one's attitude towards and investment in the body is related to suicidal behavior, arguing that body dissatisfaction contributes to a greater propensity for self-harm because a person develops disregard for the body. Body dissatisfaction and/or disregard increases the likelihood a person will view the body as an object separate from the self, making it easier to harm. Preliminary support for this idea was identified by Orbach, [D.S.] Stein, and [D.] Mirit-Har, who found that suicidal adolescents report significantly more negative attitudes and feelings toward the body, less body protection, and more body aberration than non-suicidal adolescents.

[P.] Miotto, [M.] de Coppi, [M.] Frezza, and [A.] Preti conceptually replicated Orbach et al.'s findings in a sample of Italian adolescents, finding that poor body attitudes were related to suicidal ideation for *both* males and females. Miotto et al.'s finding is important because it points to the fact that males experience disturbances in body image as well as females, suggesting that negative body image may increase risk for suicide in both sexes. More recently, Orbach et al. found that both male and female psychiatric adolescents who attempted suicide had significantly more negative body attitudes and body experiences than both psychiatric and normal control adolescents. These studies imply that suicidal adolescents have significantly more negative feelings and attitudes about their body, and are less concerned about protecting it than non-suicidal adolescents. This reduced regard for the body is what is hypothesized to increase the likelihood of engaging in self-destructive acts such as suicide, yet there are only a few studies testing this hypothesis. Of those studies examining Orbach's theory, many are limited by small sample sizes and would benefit from being replicated with a larger sample of adolescents. Another limitation to the current research is that a majority of the studies have been conducted with inpatient samples of adolescents, with mostly Israeli samples. It is necessary to determine whether findings from the current literature generalize to more diverse, non-clinical samples of adolescents.

The purpose of the current study was to test the hypothesis that negative body-image factors, as measured by the Body Investment Scale, would account for a significant, unique portion of the variance in suicidal ideation after controlling for the effects of traditional suicide risk factors in a community sample of adolescents. We also hypothesized that negative body-image factors would significantly predict suicide risk for *both* males and females.

Methods and Participants

Data from 231 American high school students were collected as part of an ongoing mental health screening conducted in a public high school. The study had IRB [institutional review board] approval from the first author's university. Participants were recruited through consent letters distributed during class time. A total of 578 letters were handed out and 334 (57.8%) were returned. While this return rate is not as high as one would like, it appears to be in line with other studies relying on school-based recruitment procedures.

Of those returned, 241 (72.2%) had parental consent to participate and 93 (27.8%) had negative parental consent. Five (2.1%) adolescents with parental consent refused to complete the study, and some students were missed due to repeated school absences. The mean age of the sample was 15.7, and a majority of the sample was female (61.4%). The ethnicity breakdown was as follows: 44.6% Caucasian, 33.8% African American, 9.5% Hispanic, 1.3% Asian, and 10.8% "other." A large portion of the sample (68%) was from a lower SES [socioeconomic status] level as indicated by participants' positive endorsement of the item: "Have you ever qualified for a reduced/free lunch program?"

A negative body image may be associated with a lack of care for the body, potentially increasing thoughts of harming the body.

Students who gave assent completed a demographic questionnaire and several self-report measures in small groups within semiprivate rooms in the school library. All measures were counterbalanced and completed within 60 min. Upon completion, each student's packet was examined for predetermined indicators of suicide risk and depression. Students requiring individual follow-up were given an appropriate referral to the school psychologist. . . .

Findings

Consistent with Orbach's theorizing that a dysfunctional view of the body increases self-destructive behaviors, we found that negative body attitudes/feelings were predictive of suicidal ideation above and beyond the effects of depression, hopelessness, and past suicidal behavior. Our findings replicate and expand those by Orbach et al. and Miotto et al., providing support for the idea that body image is an important risk factor for suicide ideation in adolescents. In addition, we found that negative body attitudes/feelings uniquely predicted suicidal ideation for *both* males and females, indicating that body image warrants inclusion in future models of suicide risk for adolescents.

In addition to body attitudes/feelings, other body-image variables such as body care should be assessed, as it also emerged as a significant predictor. It is possible that a synergistic effect among body-related constructs leads to increased risk. Adolescence is a time period during which many females and males experience dissatisfaction with their bodies. Once these negative feelings are in place, adolescents may develop a general disregard or even hate for their body. Adolescents who view their body negatively may have less investment in protecting it from harm, making suicide seem a more feasible option during times of distress, thus increasing their suicide ideation and risk for completion. This hypothesis is in line with Orbach et al.'s findings that life and death attitudes were entwined with body-image factors, and warrants further study.

A second objective of the study was to examine whether the identified risk factors would be significant for both males and females. When interactions between gender and the risk variables were considered, neither hopelessness nor gender remained as significant predictors, suggesting depression, past suicidal behavior, and body image may be more salient variables to consider. Additionally, none of the gender interactions were significant, suggesting that the risk factors identified are robust predictors for both males and females.

With regard to the body-image variables, both body attitudes/feelings and body care were found to be significant predictors of suicidal ideation for males and females. . . . The findings suggest that body attitudes/feelings may be the most robust aspect of body image associated with suicide risk, and that negative body image is not a suicide risk factor unique to females. Our finding that body care also made a significant contribution to predicting suicidal ideation provides support for Orbach's notion that a negative body image may be associated with a lack of care for the body, potentially increasing thoughts of harming the body. Additional research is needed to tease apart the multidimensional nature of body image and its relationship to suicide. In the mean time, our results further support the literature suggesting that body attitudes have strong relationships to suicidal ideation. Negative body attitudes in adolescents should be a cause for concern, especially if they are expressed in the presence of depressive symptoms or past suicidal behavior.

Future studies should strive to expand current conceptualizations of suicide risk in adolescents to include developmental phenomena . . . such as body image, attitudes, and experiences.

While our results contribute important findings, some limitations should be noted. First, because our study attempted to generalize existing findings to a non-clinical sample, the overall levels of suicide ideation were low. Second, informing participants about the referral process may have reduced willingness to report suicide-related behaviors. Additionally, our sample was predominantly female (61.4%) and Caucasian (44.6%), limiting the generalizability of the results. Lastly, our data are correlational and while they provide interesting information on relationships between variables, directionality among variables cannot be determined. Longitudinal studies are needed to examine the causal role body image or body dissatisfaction may have on risk for suicide during adolescence as well as adulthood.

Body Image Is a Factor

In conclusion, the results of the current study support the idea that body image is significantly related to suicide risk in adolescents above and beyond the effects of traditional risk factors. Negative body attitudes/feelings appear to be the most relevant element of body image associated with increased suicidality for both male and female adolescents. Aspects of body image are often overlooked in the suicide literature as potential suicide risk factors, which may be a costly oversight. Given the results of the current study, future studies should strive to expand current conceptualizations of suicide risk in adolescents to include developmental phenomena that may be unique to this age group, such as body image, attitudes, and experiences.

8

High School Athletics Participation Decreases Teen Suicide Risk

Don Sabo et al.

Don Sabo is a professor of sociology and the director of the Center for Research on Physical Activity, Sport and Health at D'Youville College in Buffalo, New York.

Adolescent involvement in athletics is often associated with increased school involvement and increased self-esteem. Generally, male and female high school athletes are thought to experience degrees of confidence and community engagement that their nonathlete peers might not. Thus, it is not surprising that, according to high school students' responses to the 1997 Youth Risk Behavior Survey, high school athletes of both sexes are less likely than their nonathlete peers to engage in suicidal thinking. While male and female high school athletes do not benefit in identical ways from their athletic involvement—and may not face decreased risk for actually attempting suicide—both groups demonstrate a decreased tendency to consider suicidal behavior.

Suicide is the third leading cause of death among US adolescents aged 15–24, with males incurring higher rates of

Don Sabo, Kathleen E. Miller, Merrill J.M. Melnick, Michael P. Farrell, and Grace M. Barnes, "High School Athletic Participation and Adolescent Suicide: A Nationwide US Study," *International Review for the Sociology of Sport*, vol 40, no. 5, 2005, pp. 5–11, 15–20. Copyright © 2008 by International Sociology of Sport Association and SAGE Publications. Republished with permission of Sage Publications, Inc., conveyed through Copyright Clearance Center, Inc.

completion than females. Although the suicide rate in the United States has remained stable over the past 40 years, the estimated rate among adolescents and young adults has nearly tripled.

Despite the seriousness of adolescent suicide, researchers have only recently begun to explore its relationship with athletic participation. Millions of US adolescents participate in school-based and community sports programs and, furthermore, athletic involvement is ostensibly associated with protective factors that have been generally found to reduce suicide risk among young people: e.g. lower rates of illicit drug use, greater social supports, reduced risk for depression. This study tests whether athletic participation is related to reduced risk for suicidal ideation [thoughts of suicide] and behavior in a nationally representative sample of US high school boys and girls.

Classical Sociology

The possibility that athletic participation is associated with lowered risk for adolescent suicide can be rooted in classical sociological thought. To the extent that adolescents become enmeshed in the social network of teammates, coaches, health professionals, family and community that emerges around organized youth sports, athletes should experience greater social integration. Development of an athlete identity and adoption of team values and goals might also lessen the contemporary adolescent experience of anomie [alienation]. [R.] Merton argued that suicide rates are likely to increase as the gap widens between a society's ideal goals and the means provided to attain them. Athletic participation may provide adolescents with the social opportunities and utilitarian skills to pursue and achieve culturally defined goals or, more subjectively, the expectation that sports involvement will help them achieve desired goals in school and in later adult life. Both of these

social-psychological processes should be associated with reduced social strain, and thus lowered suicide risk. . . .

When suicidality is conceptualized as a deviant behavior,
some contemporary theories point to social psychological factors that may be related to suicidal ideation and behavior
among teenage athletes. For example, control theory further
suggests that strong social bonds reduce individual deviance.
Athletic participation promotes the development of social
bonds within an institutional setting and the adoption of inner and outer controls during adolescence. Involvement in
sports is generally accompanied by attachment to influential
others (such as coaches and teammates) as well as reinforce-
ment of conventional beliefs and values. Moreover, a commit-
ment to organized sports gives adolescent participants something to lose. For all of the above reasons, athletic participation
should reduce the risk of suicidal ideation and behavior
among adolescents.

---

*Adolescents who construct an athletic identity . . . tend to
be rewarded with status gains within the school and . . .
greater educational and labor market success as adults.*

While it can be argued that sport involvement enhances
social integration, reduces social strain, and promotes stronger
social bonds, contemporary critical sociologists are quick to
argue that athletic participation unfolds within institutional
structures that are stratified by class, gender and race. These
processes foster access and mobility for some groups but not
others, and unequal treatment is also likely to persist after
gaining entry, e.g. historical discriminatory practices that
barred blacks and women from athletic opportunities. Athletic
participation is, therefore, related to a set of multi-faceted institutional processes in which adolescents develop identity, en-
act a variety of cultural scripts for social behavior, and build
personal and social resources. The implications of these pro-

cesses for understanding suicidal ideation and behavior still need to be addressed. In this article we highlight the potential relevance of cultural resource theory to ongoing conceptual efforts to understand suicidality in general and, in particular, variations in suicidal ideation and behavior among teenage athletes. Cultural resource theory shows promise because it integrates both exchange theory and gender theory to explain the linkages between athletic participation and adolescent health risk behavior, including suicidality.

Resource-Building

Cultural resource theory combines two key theoretical components in order to understand the relationship between sports and suicidal ideation and behavior. The first component speaks to the development of personal and social resources that buffer against suicidality. Participation in high school sports has long been a highly valued source of popularity for boys. While the sport arena was historically denied to girls, growing female sports participation since the 1970s has been accompanied by shifting attitudes toward femininity and female athleticism. Today female high school athletes, like boys, enjoy elevated popularity. The research also shows that both female and male athletes are more likely than non-athletes to be involved with school extracurricular activities and community organizations.

Parents and school officials typically perceive sports as a wholesome activity that 'builds character' and contributes to success in adult life. Through sports involvement, adolescents make friends, become more popular, and acquire college-related values and expectations. Successful development of an athletic identity may also contribute to a young person's self-efficacy, gender identity development, social acceptance, leadership skills, and upward mobility. In other words, adolescents who construct an athletic identity, both subjectively and institutionally, tend to be rewarded with status gains within the school and, to some extent, greater educational and labor

69

market success as adults. We contend that greater social integration and status attainment should be associated with lowered risk for suicidality.

Both components of cultural resource theory—resource-building and cultural scripting of gender identity—favor athletic participation as a deterrent to adolescent suicidality.

Gendered Cultural Scripts

The second component of cultural resource theory related to suicidal ideation and behavior revolves around the cultural scripting of general behavior and gender identity formation. Adolescents, who lack an extensive repertoire of personal experience, may be particularly inclined to draw upon existing cultural scripts as they strive to construct personal identities and locate themselves within social hierarchies. Though scripts may vary substantially along racial/ethnic, class, or subcultural lines, it is not difficult to identify a cluster of characteristics and behaviors that have come to be institutionalized as 'feminine' or 'masculine'. The traditional feminine cultural script or 'emphasized femininity' celebrates fragility, passivity, compliance with men's desires, and sexual receptivity, which in turn, may predispose girls to internalizing problem behaviors such as anxiety, depression, suicidality, and disordered eating. In contrast, the traditional masculine script often can prompt boys to adopt externalizing problem behaviors such as aggression and delinquency.

Sport has also been theorized as a cultural milieu in which boys, and increasingly girls, are encouraged to perceive and adopt athletic practices defined as 'masculine', thereby making sport an institutional conduit for the enactment of hegemonic masculinity [being number one]. In US sport, hegemonic masculinity emphasizes aggression, dominance-striving, conformity to authority, the devaluation of femininity, and the glorification of suffering and sacrifice. [M.A.] Messner identifies a similar clustering of manly traits at the center of media representations of the sport subculture as the 'televised sports manhood formula'; e.g. toughness, strength, hardness (avoidance of being soft), aggression, and a willingness to compromise personal health in order to win.

During the last three decades, millions of US girls have begun to participate in competitive sports, and today, young athletes of *both* sexes pursue the prevailing athletic traits and cultural practices once considered exclusively 'masculine', such as competitiveness, instrumentalism, success striving, stoicism, and aggression. As more female athletes experiment with scripts that valorize competition, goal attainment, and physical assertiveness, their identification with traditional 'femininity'—with its implications for depression, suicidality, and other internalizing characteristics—may be weakened. . . .

Both components of cultural resource theory—resource-building and cultural scripting of gender identity—favor athletic participation as a deterrent to adolescent suicidality. The logic suggests that high school athletes are less likely than their non-athlete peers to consider, plan, or attempt suicide. However, for those adolescents who do in fact attempt to kill themselves, the theoretical implications are somewhat different. Critical sociological studies of sport have showed that during the latter 20th century, men's team sports (e.g. baseball, basketball, football, hockey and rugby) reproduced cultural practices that encouraged boys to conform to hegemonic masculinity. By identifying with such hegemonically masculine traits such as violence proneness ('be tough', 'kick ass'), goal attainment ('win at all costs'), emotional inexpressivity ('suck it up'), and stoicism ('no pain, no gain') in the face of physical and emotional duress, male athletes may actually incur greater physical injury from suicide attempts. In contrast, the adoption of hegemonically masculine traits associated with the athlete script may not be associated with an increased rate of physical injury among adolescent girls. To begin with, girls typically use less violent and aggressive means than boys in their suicide attempts. Second, whereas gender identity development among boys in many sports often amplifies traits associated with hegemonic masculinity, girls' gender identity development vis-a-vis sport and the adoption of more masculine traits is weakened by cultural pressures to conform to traditional notions of femininity. Female athletes who attempt suicide, therefore, would not bring the same degree of goal-directedness, violence-proneness, and physical or emotional denial to the act as their more hegemonically masculine male athlete counterparts.

Both female and male athletes in this study reported significantly lower rates of suicidal ideation and behavior than their non-athlete counterparts.

Hypotheses

The theoretical framework outlined fostered the following hypotheses.

1. For both genders, athletes will be less likely than their non-athlete counterparts to consider, plan, and attempt suicide.

2. For both genders, higher degrees of athletic participation will be associated with reduced risk for suicidality; i.e. when compared with non-athletes, the highly involved athletes will show less risk for considering, planning and attempting suicide than moderately involved athletes.

3. Among male adolescents who attempt suicide, athletes will be at greater risk for resultant injury than their non-athlete counterparts.

4. When compared with their respective non-athlete counterparts, male athletes who attempt suicide will have
greater risk of resultant injury than female athletes who
attempt suicide. . . .

Findings

Descriptive statistics showed that both female and male athletes in this study reported significantly lower rates of suicidal
ideation and behavior than their non-athlete counterparts,
and the associations were most notable for highly involved
athletes. After controlling for the effects of age, race/ethnicity,
parental educational attainment, and school location, however,
a more nuanced set of findings resulted. Athletes of both genders were less likely than non-athletes to have considered suicide, with highly involved athletes enjoying the lowest risk.
The relationship between athletic participation and making an
actual plan for committing suicide differed by gender; only female athletes (particularly those who were highly involved)
were at less risk of planning a suicide attempt. The findings
on suicide attempts, however, yielded no significant relationships for either females or males; i.e. the reported prevalence
of suicide attempts among athletes of both sexes was not different than the rates of their non-athlete counterparts. Finally,
suicidal male athletes (especially the highly involved athletes)
were more likely than their non-athlete counterparts to report
serious injury after a suicide attempt; no differences between
suicidal female athletes and non-athletes were evident in this
regard.

These results provide mixed support for the four hypotheses. As yet, we can only speculate about the gender-specific
social, psychological, and physiological mechanisms by which
athletic participation can influence suicide risk.

The findings that athletic participation was associated with
reduced adolescent risk for considering suicide and, for girls
only, planning to commit suicide, are generally consistent with

social integration theory, structural strain theory and control theory. Sports involvement may promote greater social integration of potentially at-risk adolescents into protective social networks, and facilitate the development of personal resources for achieving socially approved goals. Athletic participation strengthens social bonds as well; as young people become more involved in athletic activities, their attachment to teammates and coaches, as well as acceptance of the normative structure of sport, becomes stronger, thereby lowering their risk for suicide.

The findings that higher rates of athletic participation for both females and males were related to some reduced suicidal ideation are also consistent with cultural resource theory. Status attainment and gender identity formation in sport may promote the formation of social bonds, ... but ... they may help adolescents to reduce social strain by providing them with the means to attain socially approved goals; e.g. parental and community approval, college/university attendance, and success in adult life. For boys, the successful pursuit of hegemonic masculinity through sport may also be said to foster upward mobility within gendered hierarchies, produce respect in accordance with prevailing gender beliefs, and foment social inclusion. As individual male athletes attempt to achieve status gains, in a collective context, their successes and failures reproduce hierarchical power relations among males and inequities between males and females. The resulting struggles of adolescent males to build resources, to form social bonds, and to manage social strain may play a role in reducing their suicidal ideation. In addition, to the extent that girls' athleticism and identification with elements of hegemonic masculinity now enhances their popularity, social inclusion, and status attainment in school and community, as it has done historically for many boys, sports participation may also reduce their risk of suicidal ideation.

The hypothesized differences between athletes and non-athletes with regard to suicidal behavior (i.e. reported attempts) were unsubstantiated among both females and males. Why would athletic participation be linked to reduced risk for ideation but not behavior? It may be that the circumstances and/or etiology of suicidal ideation differ among athletes and non-athletes. For example, extant research shows that physical activity and athletic participation are likely to lower risk for depression. It may be, however, that when teenage athletes do become depressed, it is more likely to result from an acute episode (e.g. failing to make first team or perceiving rejection by a coach) rather than a chronic condition. Future researchers might explore whether depression is more chronic among non-athletes than athletes, and whether acute or episodic depression is more prevalent among athletes than non-athletes. Chronicity might account for the higher rates of suicidal ideation among the non-athletes in our study. More research is needed to explore these social-psychological processes.

Although differences may exist in the ways that athletic participation influences the gender identity development and social integration of boys and girls, our analysis revealed several similarities between the sexes with regard to suicidal ideation and behavior. For both genders, the reported prevalence of suicidal ideation was lowest among highly involved athletes and highest among non-athletes. After controls were instituted, however, athletic participation significantly lowered only girls' risks for considering and planning suicide. Yet there were marked differences between females and males in relation to reported injury after a suicide attempt. . . .

Significance of Athletic Participation

The findings suggest three important implications for sociologists who study sport, gender, and health. First, it is important that highly involved female athletes displayed significantly lower risk for suicidal ideation than female non-athletes. Highly involved male athletes also had lower risk for considering suicide than their non-athlete male counterparts. When assessing individuals for potential suicide, clinicians often assume a continuum of risk, with increasing lethality as individuals move from considering suicide, through devising a plan for suicide, to an actual attempt. It may be important from a public health perspective, therefore, that highly involved athletes of both genders display less risk than their non-athlete counterparts at considering suicide. While future researchers must not oversimplify or overstate the associations between athletic participation and adolescent suicide risk, the preventive implications of this finding merit serious consideration by public health advocates and health planners.

We need to know more about how sport settings can operate as social vehicles for health promotion and prevention.

Second, although directional findings for lowered odds of planning a suicide in male athletes did not attain statistical significance, the overall findings were similar. Likewise, [D.R.] Brown and [C.J.] Blanton's analysis of a nationwide sample of US university students showed that athletes of both sexes reported lower rates of suicidal behavior than their non-athlete counterparts. Both gender similarities and differences appear to influence the biological, psychological, and socio-cultural processes that, in turn, inform health processes and outcomes. Future researchers need to be aware of these interactions and complexities, particularly as social forces continue to transform gender relations in sport.

Third, the finding that highly involved male athletes who attempted suicide were nearly five times as likely as male non-athletes to require medical attention has preventive implications. No person who exhibits suicidal thinking should be ignored. But teachers, school counselors, and coaches may want to pay particular attention to depressive symptoms among highly involved male athletes, since those who fall into this category are at unusually high risk for harm.

Athletic Participation Must be Further Studied

School and community-based sport programs are often regarded as extra-curricular sites for learning and character development. We need to know more about how sport settings can operate as social vehicles for health promotion and prevention. When young people become members of athletic teams, they are typically drawn into a formal health system that facilitates contact with medical professionals such as physicians, nurses, and athletic trainers. Physical examinations are required for participation and periodic check-ups and/or treatment for injuries are routine. Athletes often have access to health care professionals who can answer questions about their bodies and health-related matters. Public health planners need to assess whether the erosion of funds and social support for high school and community-based sports programs is detrimental to adolescent health. . . .

Future researchers also need to explore bio-psychosocial explanations for these findings. For example, researchers might examine possible links between physical activity and depression, a frequent correlate of suicide. [E.] Frydenberg and [R.] Lewis speculated that because sport involvement fosters positive peer relations and social integration between families and school, it helps adolescents deal with stress. Researchers might further explore the influence of social context and stress in relation to sport and adolescent suicide. More work needs done to disentangle the interfaces between athletic participation, exercise, and adolescent suicide.

Finally, sport is an institutional setting in which millions of young people interact regularly with supportive adults in ways that can influence health processes and outcomes. A greater understanding of the developmental importance of sport in adolescent subcultures will help shape effective preventive and health promotional interventions.

9

A Team Approach Is Best Suited to Addressing a Student's Suicide

Mary Finn Maples et al.

Mary Finn Maples is affiliated with the Department of Counseling and Educational Psychology at the University of Nevada–Reno.

As one counselor's words following a teen's suicide indicate, adolescent suicide is a difficult issue for school teachers, students, and community members to cope with. Grief, guilt, and uncertainty are inevitable. But, this does not mean that the possibility of teen suicide should be ignored. Rather, school staff members and concerned parents must work together as a team to develop "postvention," or after-the-fact, strategies for dealing with the emotional turbulence inevitably following from a teen suicide.

This article was prompted by a suicide by a middle school child. The school counselor who was involved [one of the authors] related the following experience:

As a helping professional working in public education for 5 years, I have dreaded confronting a few types of situations. One early fear I had was discovering and reporting child abuse. However, there was nothing I dreaded more than the possibil-

Mary Finn Maples, Jill Packman, Paul Abney, Richard F. Daugherty, John A. Casey, and Linde Pirtle, "Suicide by Teenagers in Middle School: A Postvention Team Approach," *Journal of Counseling and Development*, vol. 83, fall, 2005, p. 397–404. Copyright © 2005 The American Counseling Association. All rights reserved. Reprinted with permission. No further reproduction authorized without written permission from the American Counseling Association.

ity of dealing with a child's suicide. Unfortunately, I was tested by this challenge during my 2nd month as a middle school counselor.

Everyone—from the clinical aide who worked in the nurse's office, to the secretaries, to classroom teachers and administrators—helped the students process their grief and confusion.

Helping Others Cope

One Monday in the fall, while attending a parent meeting at the middle school where I worked, I heard my name paged over the school intercom. I was asked to report to the office immediately. Upon my arrival, I saw the stricken expression of the school vice principal. I learned she was on the phone with the local police department. While still on the phone, she communicated to all the counselors present that a student had died. As soon as she hung up, she informed us that one of our eighth-grade students (who was on my caseload, but whom I had not yet met) had died from a gunshot wound, and it was suspected that he had committed suicide. Before we could start notifying the teachers at the school, our priority was to determine whether the death was a suicide or an accident. After conferring with the police, we were informed that the death was indeed a suicide. As trained professionals, we were taught to be prepared; however, we were still enveloped by a numbing shock. Our mettle tested, we were aware that many would be relying on us to be the cornerstone of strength. We prepared to face the formidable challenge of helping others to cope.

Our first responsibility was to notify the teachers so they would not come to school and be blindsided by news of the tragedy. We felt it was important that the teachers and staff have an opportunity to prepare themselves for what would inevitably be a chaotic day full of grief, mourning, and questions. One of the counselors took responsibility for calling the teachers individually. The other counselor and I were delegated the task of calling the homes of the dead child's close friends to notify their parents. The parents were advised to talk to their children, explain what had happened, and process the tragedy as a family. The goal was to provide those we assessed as being the most affected by the news with an opportunity to grieve with family and to prepare all the students for the day ahead. . . .

The community provided support and guidance during this difficult time. Counselors from across the school district came to our site to help students process the tragedy. I called one of the professors from my counseling program at our local university, and he came to assist us. A volunteer from a crisis call center hotline also came to provide information and expertise. We set up empty classrooms to allow for group processing and individual counseling. These community members were extremely helpful to us during this time of crisis and were instrumental in identifying students who seemed to be having a particularly difficult time coping with the news of the suicide. On the basis of their observations and input, we were able to identify students in need of additional counseling and provide them with the resources they needed.

Trained counseling professionals were not the only adults who played key roles during this tough day. Other adults at our school provided comfort and support to the students. Everyone—from the clinical aide who worked in the nurse's office, to the secretaries, to classroom teachers and administrators—helped the students process their grief and confusion. . . .

Along with the appropriate expressions of grief displayed by the students, we found ourselves confronted with some that were not appropriate in a public school. Because we were concerned about "copycat" suicides, we wanted the students to be allowed to grieve but did not want to glorify the suicide.

For example, posters bearing the deceased student's picture stating that the student would be missed were removed from the halls and memorial paraphernalia were removed from the locker of the student who committed suicide. The students were angry and resented this decision. They believed it was respectful to remember the student in this way. However, with the support from the counseling staff, the administrators maintained their position, and memorializing at school was kept to a minimum. . . .

Continuing Responsibilities

Our responsibilities in the wake of this tragedy did not end with this boy's burial. . . . More and more students began coming forward to talk to their friends, teachers, and counselors about suicidal ideation [thoughts]. We were in constant contact with the parents of students who expressed thoughts of suicide and made several referrals to hospitals that provided inpatient counseling and help with depression. Some of the students who were feeling depressed said that the suicide had brought to the surface feelings of sadness and grief they had experienced in the past when other family members or friends had died. Some students who had friends who had committed suicide in previous years were feeling scared, confused, and personally responsible for the most recent suicide.

I facilitated two grief and loss support groups, one for the best friends of the student who committed suicide and one for students who were experiencing grief as the result of the deaths of parents, cousins, and friends as well as the recent suicide. We focused on the stages of grief, coping skills, and the students' personal feelings and experiences in relationship to the deaths in their lives. . . .

The lives of the students and staff at our middle school will never be the same since one of the eighth graders took his own life. The student was a friend, a teammate, and a member of the middle school graduating class of 2003. I believe strongly in our *prevention* efforts at this school and pray that no school is ever again confronted with such a tragedy. However, I have lost my naïveté and know that crises like the one we faced in the fall occur more often than we would like to imagine.

The foregoing experience of a new counselor, simultaneously poignant and accountable, suggests that there is a high price to pay for gaining this valuable experience. Counselors, in conjunction with other school staff, can discuss possible ways of handling a crisis situation at school more efficiently, but all the plans possible can never answer the question, "How do children reach such desperation as to make the choice to die?" How can children who have only been alive for 12 to 14 years want to end their lives? The experience of survivor's pain following the loss of a child through illness, disease, or accident is dreadful and powerful. Psychological pain due to the death of a child who has chosen to die is indescribable. From the counselor's narrative, it appeared that future programs for prevention and intervention were planned at her school. However, as with many cases of suicide, no programs or services had been discussed or planned that could be used in the immediate aftermath of a suicide. Hence, the purpose of this article.

Youth Suicide Is Different

The factors indicative of youth who are at risk of suicide differ dramatically from those of adult suicide. Adolescence is the most volatile period of transition in the human growth cycle. . . .

The years spent in middle school represent a remarkable time of change for children: They face new schools, new teachers, often new friends (and enemies), new academic challenges, and emotional turmoil brought on by puberty. Because of such rapid changes, middle schoolers often have difficulty understanding their own unpredictable feelings. This lack of understanding and subsequent confusion and frustration may have tragic conclusions if proper identification of potential suicide-risk students and steps to assist these students in their adjustment phases are not implemented. . . .

Most adolescents experience some problems [with low self-esteem, depression, irritability or social withdrawal] at some point. It is, however, crucial that school counselors, administrators, parents, and other significant adults recognize changes in behavior, moods, choice of friends, and grades. Also of critical importance is the duration of the child's struggles with these warning signs. Although an impending suicide attempt may be indicated if an adolescent experiences these struggles for an extended period of time, a caring adult can still offer support and guidance in a child's life during a crisis whether or not it is believed that a suicide attempt is a possible outcome. . . .

We strongly suggest that parents be involved in a postvention team.

Need for Postvention Considerations

According to statistics from the Children's Defense Fund, five children under the age of 20 commit suicide every day. These alarming statistics suggest that "as school counselors [and administrators and parents] each of us will most likely experience the tragedy of a student suicide at some point in our careers". In writing of the counselor's role in the postvention phase of a student suicide, [R.] Parsons has suggested several considerations:

- Consider that there may be one suicide, but there are many victims

- Deal with guilt and destructive self-doubts

- Assist in the student's acknowledgment of feelings

- Implement postvention, not denial

- Focus on the student's response to life

- Clarify that there are both endings and beginnings

Each of these issues is a reason in itself to attend seriously to the aftermath of suicide. For example, consider the public attention given to the phenomenon of "copycat" suicides. According to [K.] Dunne-Maxim and [M.] Underwood, there are many debilitating effects that may result from a student's suicide. Although [R.] Parsons recommended that counselors, teachers, and administrators "move in a decisive, directed and thoughtful way when confronted by the reality of a student suicide", we strongly suggest that parents be involved in a postvention team. [S.] Poland offered specific guidelines that may be used to develop and train a team to deal with the postvention phase of a teen suicide. His plan is one suggested by the American Association of Suicidology:

1. Plan in advance of any crisis.

2. Select and train a crisis team.

3. Verify report of suicide from collaboration with the medical examiner, police, and family of the deceased.

4. Do not dismiss school or encourage funeral attendance during school hours.

5. Do not dedicate a memorial (e.g., yearbook, tree, bench).

6. Do contribute to a suicide prevention effort on behalf of the schools or the community.

7. Do contact the family, apprise them of the school's intervention efforts, and assist with funeral arrangements.

8. Do not release information in a large assembly or over intercom systems. Disseminate information in informal meetings with individual groups of faculty, students, and parents. *Always* be truthful.

9. Follow the suicide victim's classes throughout the day to provide opportunity for discussion and counseling.

10. Arrange for counseling rooms in the school building and provide individual and group counseling.

11. Collaborate with media, law enforcement, and community agencies.

12. Points to emphasize with media and parents: prevention, no one thing or person is to blame, help is available.

13. Provide counseling or discussion opportunities for the faculty.

Carol Watkins has suggested a comprehensive approach to prevention, intervention, and postvention related to youth suicide. Although she recommended involving the school community (i.e., counselors, teachers, administrators, and students) in the postvention phase, we believe that a major resource has been omitted, that of parents—particularly those who are survivors of a child who took his or her life or, perhaps, a close relative of one. This is the premise that was the basis for our recommendation of the CAPT (counselors, administrators, parents, and teachers) Team Approach.

Different responses may be appropriate for different students who are at various stages of the postvention process.

The CAPT Team Approach

[R.] Roberts, [W.] Lepkowski, and [K.] Davidson recommended the development of a team, establishment of procedures, arrangement of supports, and monitoring of progress when dealing with the aftermath of teen suicide. Roberts et al. have recommended that the team be organized to represent a cross section of the community. However, in our approach we specify that the members of a cross-sectional team be limited to counselors, administrators, parents, and teachers who have been directly involved with a teen suicide and, perhaps, accepting friends and fellow students as participants when appropriate. Roberts et al. called their model the T.E.A.M. Program, outlined as follows:

T: Developing a Team

1. Who will make up the members of the team?
2. Who will be the team leader?
3. How will individuals' differing strengths be channeled into their respective assignments?
4. Are all the tasks assigned and covered (e.g., phone operator, family and media liaison, group leader)?
5. Is the postvention plan written and approved?
6. When will the in-service meetings be provided, and what will they cover?

E: Establishing Procedures

1. How will we notify all staff members in the event of a suicide?
2. How and when will we announce the death to the students?
3. Which team member will deal with the news media?
4. What information do we want to release?
5. What does the family want?
6. What does the school district allow?
7. How will the memorial activities be organized and communicated?

A: Arranging Supports

1. How will support groups be run? (e.g., Who will lead? How long will the group meetings last? Who will participate?)

2. When will debriefing meetings be held, and who will lead them?

3. What team member will be the liaison with the family?

M: Monitoring Progress

1. How will we monitor those who are at risk of suicide?

2. What long-term community support for those at risk should be provided?

3. How will the school remain prepared for a student suicide?

It should be noted that the T.E.A.M. Program developed by Roberts et al. and modified by us as the CAPT Team Approach could be adapted to include the prevention and intervention phases of dealing with teen suicides. We recommend that these issues be resolved for each school before the school is faced with a crisis. Attempting to assemble a CAPT team in the chaotic aftermath of a suicide is neither prudent nor realistic.

A Four-Stage Model

The success of the CAPT team members is dependent, in part, on their knowledge of and skills related to the postvention process. Teaching the four-stage model, developed in part from the work of [L.M.] Brammer, [P.] Abrego, and [E.] Shostrom, may enhance their expertise in this area. Although the stages are not necessarily sequential, knowledge of each stage may help remind the CAPT team members that different responses may be appropriate for different students who are at various stages of the postvention process. It is also vital to remember that stages are not time limited (i.e., the duration of each stage varies).

Stage 1: Shock and disorganization. There is often an initial numbness and denial when an individual first hears the news of a suicide. Reactions such as "There must be some mistake!" or "No, it's not possible, he/she of all people would never do such a thing!" are common. An effective way for the CAPT team members to approach this first stage, regardless of theoretical orientation, is to draw on the core conditions by being supportive, nonjudgmental, and caring and to actively listen to concerns. The shock to a student is often accompanied by a feeling of disorganization, which can interfere with normal daily functions (e.g., eating and sleeping). In this situation, both medical and behavioral strategies are helpful. In the case described at the beginning of the article, several students were referred to the nurse or their family doctor, who then prescribed sleeping aids. Moreover, the counselor taught the students relaxation strategies, using visual imagery and progressive muscular relaxation, to behaviorally help anxious students focus on relaxing at scheduled bedtimes and at mealtimes.

Stage 2: Expressions of anguish and remorse. The deep pain over the loss of a student through suicide, which may include guilt and regret, is common: "Oh, why didn't I see the signs? Why didn't I pick up on his or her feelings?" This stage is sometimes called the "stage of increased vulnerability" because feelings are close to the surface and easily triggered by numerous stimuli.... CAPT team members may be taught, at this stage, to help students develop cognitive-behavioral strategies for coping. One example of a cognitive-behavioral strategy is "thought stoppage," where the guilt-ridden person commands himself or herself to "stop reliving the past." A substitute thought can be developed and practiced, such as a "mental videotape" of a more positive interaction between the individual and the deceased....

Prevention of suicide is ideal, but when one occurs, having a plan of action for notifying faculty and staff, the students, and community support personnel is essential.

Stage 3: Exploring the meaning of the loss. This stage usually does not set in until after the initial heightened level of activity surrounding the suicide has subsided. Thus, on the 1st day after the funeral, large number of students might return to daily routines, but internally, they may have recurring moments of reflection on the loss and its meaning for their lives. This stage is characterized by a questioning process: "Why am I in school?" "What is the meaning of life, anyway?" "Who gives a damn about math and language arts when ____ is dead?" It is common for well-intentioned persons to want to "cheer up" the mourning person by taking his or her mind off the loss saying, "Hey, let's go see a movie!" CAPT team members can be educated about the value of assisting the student, at this stage, with his or her existential search. Setting up ongoing, scheduled counseling groups where serious, heart-to-heart talks can occur is one such intervention described in the earlier case study. (These counseling groups can also provide realistic feedback opportunities to teens who construct unrealistic and imaginary audiences. . . .) Bibliotherapy [reading helpful texts] (in conjunction with the school librarian) and journal writing (shared with trusted members within the counseling group) can be useful at this stage. . . .

Stage 4: Emergence toward new goals. A successful resolution of the existential search described in Stage 3 can yield increased motivation and enthusiasm to pursue newly established goals. For example, fellow athletes may have decided to dedicate the remainder of the season to the memory of the deceased. Some friends, having come through the first three stages together, may vow to stay lifelong friends and always share their troubles instead of keeping them inside. More long-term goals, such as family, school, or career achievement, are also commonly expressed during this stage. CAPT team members can be trained to help students embrace these goals, identify realistic strategies to help achieve them, and develop timelines and periodic checkpoints to reassess these goals over time. . . .

Implications for Counselors

Although no counselor wants to be faced with the suicide of a student, planning for such an event can alleviate some of the stress that results if and when a suicide occurs. Prevention of suicide is ideal, but when one occurs, having a plan of action for notifying faculty and staff, the students, and community support personnel is essential. With the CAPT Team Approach in place, the counselor is not lost and overwhelmed about what to do: The decisions have already been made. Postvention support is in place and all those involved know their role. The CAPT Team Approach allows counselors and administrators to rely on decisions made while the full body of resources is known and there is time to explore the best options for a worst-case scenario.

10

The Merits of Suicide Risk
Tests Are Debatable

Shankar Vedantam

Shankar Vedantam is a Washington Post *staff writer.*

The use of suicide screening tests is on the rise in U.S. schools. Yet, there is little hard evidence that such screening works to prevent teen suicide. While proponents of suicide screening argue that mental health issues need as much attention as physical health issues, opponents view screening tests as expensive tools of the pharmaceutical industry. Ultimately, the uncertainty and controversy surrounding suicide screening in U.S. schools might point to the need for rethinking and reformatting the tests themselves.

A growing number of U.S. schools are screening teenagers for suicidal tendencies or signs of mental illness, triggering a debate between those who seek to reduce the toll of youthful suicides and others who say the tests are unreliable and intrude on family privacy.

The trend is being aggressively promoted by those who say screening can reduce the tragedy of the more than 1,700 suicides committed by children and adolescents each year in the United States. Many of the most passionate supporters have lost children to suicide—among them Sen. Gordon Smith (R-Ore.), whose son Garrett died in 2003. One screening program, TeenScreen, developed by Columbia University, has been administered to more than 150,000 children in 42 states and the District [of Columbia]. The state of New York plans to start screening 400,000 children a year, and the federal government is directing tens of millions of dollars to expand screening nationwide.

Use of Tests Growing

Use of the psychological evaluations is growing even though there is little hard evidence that they prevent suicides. A panel of government experts concluded [in 2004] that the evidence to justify suicide screening was weak and that such programs, although well intentioned, had potential adverse consequences.

The growing use of screening has coincided with a rapid increase in the number of youngsters being prescribed powerful antipsychotic medications such as Risperdal and Zyprexa that have not been specifically approved for use by children. There was a fivefold increase in the use of these drugs in children between 1993 and 2002, according to one analysis published [in June 2006] in the *Archives of General Psychiatry*, and a 73 percent increase in such prescriptions between 2001 and 2005, according to Medco, a firm that manages pharmacy benefits.

An Emotional Debate

Proponents of screening say that it is no different than having health checkups or visiting a dentist, and that the potential benefits are incalculable. After Smith's son killed himself, the Republican bucked the objections of several conservative groups to push into a law an $82 million effort to expand programs such as TeenScreen. "Without any doubt, had Teen-Screen been available to us as Garrett's parents, I am convinced we would have been empowered to save his life," Smith said in an interview. "Logic tells me the more you know, the more you are able to help."

Garrett Smith died one day shy of his 22nd birthday. He had seen a psychiatrist shortly before he committed suicide and was given a prescription for an antidepressant. Sen. Smith said the family did not know whether Garrett took the medication. Later, Smith said, several experts concluded that Garrett probably had bipolar disorder, also known as manic-depression. Antidepressants are not recommended for this condition, and Smith said his son had probably concealed his symptoms during his single visit with the psychiatrist. Still, he said, if the family had known that Garrett had bipolar disorder, they could have acted years earlier.

Suicide screening can reveal problems that parents may never detect.

The controversy over screening has become emotional. Opponents say such programs have turned into fronts for the pharmaceutical industry to boost sales. Advocates, meanwhile, say those against screening are often driven by anti-psychiatry ideologies such as Scientology. "It is industrial psychology at its worst," said Michael D. Ostrolenk, a family therapist with the Eagle Forum, a conservative group founded by commentator Phyllis Schlafly. "We think it is inappropriate to turn state schools into laboratories for psychiatry." He added that the group is also concerned that screening violates family privacy.

But screening has wide support among both Republicans and Democrats. In 2004, President [George W.] Bush signed into law the Garrett Lee Smith Memorial Act to boost funding for suicide screening, and the President's New Freedom Commission on Mental Health has been broadly supportive.

The debate over screening also turns on the scientific paradoxes of suicide. It is rare enough that it is difficult to study by conventional scientific trials, but common enough to claim the lives of more than 30,000 Americans each year—far more than those who die by homicide. There were 1,737 suicides by children and adolescents in 2003, the last year for which national statistics are available. Among those younger than 20, the suicide rate is 2.14 per 100,000, a fraction of the 14.6 per 100,000 rate for those older than 50. But national surveys suggest that about 1 in 12 high school students tries to harm himself or herself each year with an eye to committing suicide.

Because suicide victims often turn out to have had mental disorders such as depression and bipolar disorder, David Shaffer of Columbia University, who developed the TeenScreen questionnaire, and other specialists say identifying and treating youngsters with such disorders may reduce the number of suicides. "If the only product of screening was to predict who is going to commit suicide you could argue about its utility," he said. "But the risk factors for suicide are other treatable psychiatric disorders."

Besides cost and intrusiveness, [screening carries] a risk of harm in terms of stigmatization.

Laurie Flynn, national executive director for TeenScreen, the largest of several such programs nationwide, said annual physical exams are less likely than mental health checkups to reveal problems. Moreover, she said, suicide screening can reveal problems that parents may never detect. Flynn's daughter attempted suicide when she was 17. When the school phoned Flynn with the news, she said, her initial reaction was "You have the wrong number."

Shaffer and Flynn said the goal is not to put children on medication but to alert parents to a problem, which they can then discuss with a pediatrician, a psychiatrist or a clergy member. Flynn said TeenScreen is supported by private donors and receives no money from the drug industry. (Much of the initial funding came from the late William J. Ruane, a former board member of The Washington Post Co.) Shaffer said the screening test he developed is now in the public domain and he does not profit from its use. . . .

Although the argument that treating mental disorders would reduce suicide is intuitively appealing, the U.S. Preventive Services Task Force, a federal panel of independent experts, concluded in 2004 that there was insufficient evidence either for or against general physicians screening the public for suicide risk. Ned Calonge, chairman of the task force, established to assess the evidence for various disease-prevention strategies, said the panel would reach the same conclusion today. "Whether or not we like to admit it, there are no interventions that have no harms," said Calonge, who is also chief medical officer for the Colorado Department of Public Health and Environment. There is weak evidence that screening can distinguish people who will commit suicide from those who will not, he said. And screening inevitably leads to treating some people who do not need it. Such interventions have consequences beyond side effects from drugs or other treatments, he said. Unnecessary care drives up the cost of insurance, causing some people to lose coverage altogether. For every 1 percent increase in premiums in Colorado, Calonge calculated, 2,500 people lose their health insurance. . . .

More Effective Tools Needed

Steven E. Hyman, a former director of the National Institute of Mental Health and now provost at Harvard University, said he favors developing screening questionnaires and treatments for children to reduce the number of suicides, but he is skeptical that such tools currently exist. "By and large, brief diagnostic tests—especially doing broad screening in children— are not well validated, and one has to be concerned about missing real illness or, conversely, interpreting transient life troubles as a mental illness requiring intervention," Hyman said. "It doesn't mean ignorance is good," he added. "But if your instrument is poor, or you don't know how to intervene to prevent a condition like suicide, there is actually a risk of harm. Besides cost and intrusiveness, there is a risk of harm in terms of stigmatization, but also interventions that backfire."

11

The Link Between Antidepressants and Teen Suicide Is Controversial

Benedict Carey

Benedict Carey is a contributor to the International Herald Tribune

Since the late 1980s, debate has raged concerning the prescription of antidepressants to children and adolescents. While some have argued that antidepressants increase suicide risk in young people, others have interpreted rising teen suicide rates as the result of antidepressant restrictions. For both the Food and Drug Administration and concerned parents, armed with few definitive scientific findings to consult, this debate continues to raise questions regarding the ethics and economics of psychopharmacology.

U.S. public health officials, psychiatrists, grieving parents, outraged former patients and others are addressing the most bitterly divisive question in psychiatry: Do the drugs that doctors prescribe to relieve depression make some people more likely to commit suicide? [In December 2006] the Food and Drug Administration decided to convene a government panel for the first time since 2004 to consider the question.

Impassioned testimony [in 2004] led the agency to require antidepressant drugs to carry strong warnings that they could increase suicidal thinking or behavior in some children and adolescents. Now the agency is considering whether to require similar warnings for adult patients.

At one level, the debate is about science, which has not provided clear answers.

Roots of the Debate

The controversy began in the late 1980s, soon after Prozac was introduced as the first in a new generation of antidepressants. Over the next 15 years, the debate came to transcend questions about side effects and labeling. It became a clash of cultures. Psychiatrists say the debate has scared patients and their families away from the very medications that could save their lives. Critics say psychiatry relies too much on drugs and on drug company money that pose a danger to public health.

"It's like a religious war," said Edward Shorter, a medical historian at the University of Toronto who is the author of the definitive "History of Psychiatry." "The only time I can remember when people argued over an issue with this kind of fervor," Shorter said, "was back in the 1960s and 1970s, when scientists were challenging psychoanalysis."

Fervor Spreading

The fervor has spread beyond academia. Family doctors and psychiatrists in private practice have more trouble than ever getting their depressed patients to try medication. Dr. Andrew Leon, a psychiatric researcher at Weill Medical College of Cornell University who is a paid scientific adviser for the pharmaceutical industry and the government, was a member of the 2004 panel and was on the panel conducting the hearing [in 2006]. "Sitting up there and having the public yell that you're killing their children is no fun," he said. "But I suppose that has become a part of the process now."

At one level, the debate is about science, which has not provided clear answers. Studies linking antidepressant use to suicide rates appear to point in opposite directions. "The bitterness or confusion, at least within academia, stems from divisions over what the evidence means," Dr. David Healy, a psychiatrist at the University of Cardiff in Wales, wrote in an e-mail message. Healy, who has argued that the suicide risk is higher than psychiatrists have acknowledged, has worked for drug makers and for plaintiffs' lawyers in cases brought against pharmaceutical companies.

Food and Drug Administration scientists who analyzed data from drug trials reported that adults under 25 who took antidepressants were more than twice as likely as those who took dummy pills to report having made suicide attempts or preparations for suicide, about the same increase in risk found in minors. But other studies have found that adolescent suicide rates, which began a steady decline in the 1990s as Prozac and its relatives became widely used, tend to be low in areas of the country where antidepressants are most widely prescribed. Autopsy studies of adolescents who committed suicide found that few had antidepressants in their system, Leon said.

The Continuing Controversy

The climate surrounding the issue changed drastically in late 2003 when British regulators, after reviewing previously unpublished data from drug company trials, effectively banned the use of most antidepressants in children and adolescents, citing a possible suicide risk. [But] researchers in the Netherlands reported [in December 2006] that the suicide rate in children and adolescents had increased by more than 40 percent since 2003, when prescription rates of antidepressants began to drop. Many psychiatrists interpret such findings as evidence that benefits of antidepressants far outweigh the risks, and say they worry about the fact that prescriptions by U.S.

doctors have dropped since 2003. "This is evidence that our worst fears could come true, that these labeling changes and reductions in prescriptions are in fact having an adverse impact on suicide rates," said Kelly Posner, an assistant professor of child psychiatry at Columbia University and the New York State Psychiatric Institute.

But others like Healy say the establishment has been in denial about the drugs' most serious side effects, in part because of the influence of drug company money. Sara Bostock of Atherton, California, was on the witness list in 2004 and again [in 2006]. Her daughter committed suicide at age 25, shortly after starting to take the antidepressant Paxil. "All along, it has been too easy to blame the victim, or the underlying disease, without acknowledging that there might be some kind of synergistic effect between the drugs and whatever problems the person has," she said.

Organizations to Contact

The editors have compiled the following list of organizations concerned with the issues debated in this book. The descriptions are derived from materials provided by the organizations. All have publications or information available for interested readers. The list was compiled on the date of publication of the present volume; the information provided here may change. Be aware that many organizations take several weeks or longer to respond to inquiries, so allow as much time as possible.

American Association of Suicidology (AAS)
5221 Wisconsin Ave. NW, Washington, DC   20015
(202) 237-2280 • fax: (202) 237-2282
e-mail: info@suicidology.org
Web site: www.suicidology.org

The association is one of the largest suicide prevention organizations in the United States. It promotes the view that suicidal thoughts are almost always a symptom of depression and that suicide is almost never a rational decision. In addition to suicide prevention, AAS also works to increase public awareness about suicide and to help those grieving the loss of a loved one to suicide. The association publishes the quarterly newsletters *American Association of Suicidology—Newslink* and *Surviving Suicide* and the quarterly journal *Suicide and Life Threatening Behavior*.

American Foundation for Suicide Prevention (AFSP)
120 Wall St., 22nd Floor, New York, NY   10005
(888) 333-2377 • fax: (212) 363-6237
e-mail: inquiry@afsp.org
Web site: www.afsp.org

Formerly known as the American Suicide Foundation, the AFSP supports scientific research on depression and suicide, educates the public and professionals on the recognition and treatment of depressed and suicidal individuals, and provides support programs for those coping with the loss of a loved one to suicide. AFSP publishes the newsletter *Lifesavers*.

American Psychiatric Association (APA)
1000 Wilson Blvd., Suite 1825, Arlington, VA   22209
(703) 907-7300
e-mail: apa@psych.org
Web site: www.psych.org

An organization of psychiatrists dedicated to studying the nature, treatment, and prevention of mental disorders, the APA helps create mental health policies, distributes information about psychiatry, and promotes psychiatric research and education. It publishes the *American Journal of Psychiatry* and *Psychiatric News* monthly.

American Psychological Association (APA)
750 First St. NE, Washington, DC   20002-4242
(202) 336-5500
e-mail: public.affairs@apa.org
Web site: www.apa.org

This professional organization for psychologists aims to "advance psychology as a science, as a profession, and as a means of promoting human welfare." It produces numerous publications, including the book *Adolescent Suicide: Assessment and Intervention*, the report "Researcher Links Perfectionism in High Achievers with Depression and Suicide," and the online guide *Warning Signs: A Violence Prevention Guide for Youth*.

Canadian Association for Suicide Prevention (CASP)
870 Portage Ave., Winnipeg, MB   R3G 0P1
   Canada
(204) 784-4073 • fax: (204) 772-7998
e-mail: casp@casp-acps.ca
Web site: www.suicideprevention.ca

CASP organizes annual conferences and educational programs on suicide prevention. It publishes the newsletter *CASP News* three times a year and the booklet *Suicide Prevention in Canadian Schools*.

Depression and Bipolar Support Alliance
730 N. Franklin St., Suite 501, Chicago, IL   60654-7225
(800) 826-3632 • fax: (312) 642-7243
Web site: www.ndmda.org

The Depression and Bipolar Support Alliance provides support and advocacy for patients with depression and bipolar disorder. It offers those living with mental illness the opportunity to participate in peer-based, recovery-centered, and empowerment-focused treatment options. It publishes the quarterly *Outreach* and various books and brochures.

International Foundation for Research and Education on Depression (iFred)
PO Box 17598, Baltimore, MD   21297-1598
(410) 268-0044 • fax: (443) 782-0739
e-mail: info@ifred.org
Web site: www.ifred.org

The International Foundation for Research and Education on Depression is one of few organizations concerned with researching the causes of depression, and helping those coping with depression, on an international scale. Through education and destigmatization efforts, iFred promotes both the general recognition that depression co-occurs with other illnesses, and the worldwide conviction that depression can be effectively and sensitively treated. It has produced flyers outlining the effects of depression on both individuals and businesses, and has launched the Field of Hope campaign aimed at illustrating the frequency with which depression is diagnosed.

The Jason Foundation, Inc.
181 E. Main St., Jefferson Bldg., Suite 5
Hendersonville, TN   37075
e-mail: info@jasonfoundation.com
Web site: www.jasonfoundation.com

The Jason Foundation is dedicated to educating students, teachers, and community organizations about the risk of teen suicide. It operates a crisis hotline aimed at assisting individuals in need of immediate help and creates multimedia resource packages designed for larger educational efforts. The Jason Foundation produces the "A Promise for Tomorrow" education curriculum, which promotes teen suicide awareness and prevention among seventh through twelfth graders, as well as the *Community Assistance Resource Line* (CARL) informational brochure.

The Jed Foundation
583 Broadway, Suite 8B, New York, NY   10012
(212) 647-7544 • fax: (320) 210-6089
Web site: www.jedfoundation.org

The Jed Foundation is a charitable organization concerned with reducing suicide among U.S. college and university students. Established in 2000 by two parents mourning the suicide death of their twenty-year-old son, it raises awareness of suicide deaths on college campuses and forges connections between academic communities researching teen suicide and higher education professionals directly connected with college-aged students. The Jed Foundation developed Ulifeline, an Internet-based resource for students struggling with depression and stress, and has developed multiple educational programs, such as Campus Care, aimed at campuswide education and prevention.

National Alliance for the Mentally Ill (NAMI)
2107 Wilson Blvd., Suite 300, Arlington, VA   22201-3042
(703) 524-7600 • fax: (703) 524-9094
Web site: www.nami.org

NAMI is a consumer advocacy and support organization composed largely of family members of people with severe mental illnesses such as schizophrenia, bipolar disorder, and depression. The alliance adheres to the position that severe mental illnesses are biological brain diseases and that mentally ill people should not be blamed or stigmatized for their conditions. NAMI favors increased government funding for research, treatment, and community services for the mentally ill. Its publications include the bimonthly newsletter *NAMI Advocate*, as well as various brochures, handbooks, and policy recommendations.

Samaritans
PO Box 9090, Stirling   FK8 2SA
  UK
+44 (0)8457 909090
e-mail: jo@samaritans.org
Web site: www.samaritans.org.uk

Samaritans is the largest suicide prevention organization in the world. Established in England in 1953, the organization now has branches in at least forty-four nations throughout the world. The group's volunteers provide counseling and other assistance to suicidal and despondent individuals. In addition, Samaritans publishes the booklets *Teen Suicide Information and Guidelines for Parents* and *The Suicidal Student: A Guide for Educators.*

SA\VE—Suicide Awareness\Voices of Education
8120 Penn Ave. South, Suite 470, Bloomington, MN   55431
(952) 946-7998
Web site: www.save.org

SA\VE works to prevent suicide and to help those grieving after the suicide of a loved one. Its members believe that brain diseases, such as depression, should be detected and treated promptly because they can result in suicide. In addition to pamphlets and the book *Suicide Survivors: A Guide for Those Left Behind*, the organization publishes the quarterly newsletter *Voices.*

Suicide Information and Education Centre (SIEC)
#201, 1615 Tenth Ave. SW, Calgary, AB   T3C 0J7
  Canada
(403) 245-3900 • fax: (403) 245-0299

e-mail: siec@siec.ca
Web site: www.siec.ca

The Suicide Information and Education Centre acquires and distributes information on suicide prevention. It maintains a computerized database, a free mailing list, and a document delivery service. It publishes the quarterly *SIEC Alert* and the monthly *SIEC Feature of the Month Bulletin*.

Youth Suicide Prevention Program (YSPP)
444 NE Ravenna Blvd., Suite 401, Seattle, WA 98115
(206) 297-5922 • fax: (206) 297-0818
e-mail: info@yspp.org
Web site: www.yspp.org

The Youth Suicide Prevention Program is firmly dedicated to reducing the number of teen suicides mourned each year. Focusing on public awareness, training, and community action, it prioritizes awareness and education. YSPP publishes a quarterly newsletter and runs a two-day education and intervention training called ASIST.

Bibliography

Books

David Cox and Candy Arrington · *Aftershock: Help, Hope, and Healing in the Wake of Suicide.* Nashville: Broadman and Holman, 2003.

Marion Crook · *Out of the Darkness: Teens Talk About Suicide.* Vancouver, BC: Arsenal Pulp Press, 2004.

Thomas P. Gullotta and Gerald R. Adams, eds. · *Handbook of Adolescent Behavioral Problems: Evidence-Based Approaches to Prevention and Treatment.* New York: Springer, 2005.

Peter M. Gutierrez and Augustine Osman · *Adolescent Suicide: An Integrated Approach to the Assessment of Risk and Protective Factors.* DeKalb: Northern Illinois University Press, 2008.

Robert A. King and Alan Apter, eds. · *Suicide in Children and Adolescents.* Cambridge: Cambridge University Press, 2003.

Kate Sofronoff, Lenard Dalgliesh, and Robert Kosky · *Out of Options: A Cognitive Model of Adolescent Suicide and Risk-Taking.* Cambridge: Cambridge University Press, 2005.

Anthony Spirito and James C. Overholser, eds. · *Evaluating and Treating Adolescent Suicide Attempters: From Research to Practice.* San Diego: Academic Press, 2003.

Periodicals

E. Baca-Garcia, M.M. Perez-Rodriguez, J.J. Mann, and M.A. Oquendo — "Suicidal Behavior in Young Women," *Psychiatric Clinics of North America*, vol. 31, no. 2, 2008.

L. Biddle, J. Donovan, K. Hawton, N. Kapur, and D. Gunnell — "Suicide and the Internet," *British Medical Journal*, vol. 336, no. 7648, 2008.

R.M. Bossarte, T.R. Simon, and M.H. Swahn — "Clustering of Adolescent Dating Violence, Peer Violence, and Suicidal Behavior," *Journal of Interpersonal Violence*, vol. 23, no. 6, 2008.

R.D. Everall, K.E. Bostik, and B.L. Paulson — "I'm Sick of Being Me: Developmental Themes in a Suicidal Adolescent," *Adolescence*, vol. 40, no. 160, 2005.

A. Haas et al. — "An Interactive Web-Based Method of Outreach to College Students at Risk for Suicide," *Journal of American College Health*, vol. 57, no. 1, 2008.

Jochen Hardt, Jeffrey G. Johnson, Elizabeth A. Courtney, and Jitender Sareen — "Childhood Adversities Associated with Risk for Suicidal Behavior," *Psychiatric Times*, June 1, 2006.

Christopher D. Houck, Wendy Hadley, Celia M. Lescano, David Pugatch, and Larry K. Brown
"Suicide Attempt and Sexual Risk Behavior: Relationship Among Adolescents," *Archives of Suicide Research*, vol. 12, no. 1, 2008.

Cheryl A. King and Christopher R. Merchant
"Social and Interpersonal Factors Relating to Adolescent Suicidality: A Review of the Literature," *Archives of Suicide Research*, vol. 12, no. 3, 2008.

Keith A. King
"Practical Strategies for Preventing Adolescent Suicide," *School Nurse News*, vol. 25, no. 2, 2008.

S.D. Molock, S. Matlin, C. Barksdale, R. Puri, and J. Lyles
"Developing Suicide Prevention Programs for African American Youth in African American Churches," *Suicide and Life-Threatening Behavior*, vol. 38, no. 3, 2008.

Patricia Petralia
"To Prevent Teen Suicide, Understand It," *Washington Post*, February 15, 2007.

J. Scourfield, K. Roen, and L. McDermott
"Lesbian, Gay, Bisexual and Transgender Young People's Experiences of Distress: Resilience, Ambivalence and Self-Destructive Behaviour," *Health & Social Care in the Community*, vol. 16, no. 3, 2008.

Shankar Vedantam
"Drugs Raise Risk of Suicide; Analysis of Data Adds to Concerns On Antidepressants," *Washington Post*, February 18, 2005.

Karen Dineen
Wagner

"Update on Antidepressants and
Suicidality," *Psychiatric Times*, July 1,
2007.

Jacki L.
Waldvogel,
Martha Rueter,
and Charles N.
Oberg

"Adolescent Suicide: Risk Factors and
Prevention Strategies," *Current
Problems in Pediatric and Adolescent
Health Care*, vol. 38, no. 4, 2008.

N.E. Walls, S.
Freedenthal, and
H. Wisneski

"Suicidal Ideation and Attempts
Among Sexual Minority Youths
Receiving Social Services," *Social
Work*, vol. 53, no. 1, 2008.

L.H. Zayas and
A.M. Pilat

"Suicidal Behavior in Latinas:
Explanatory Cultural Factors and
Implications for Intervention,"
*Suicide and Life-Threatening
Behavior*, vol. 38, no. 3, 2008.

Internet Sources

American
Academy of
Pediatrics

"Some Things You Should Know
About Preventing Teen Suicide."
www.aap.org/advocacy/
childhealthmonth/
prevteensuicide.htm.

American
Psychiatric
Association

"Let's Talk Facts About Teen Suicide."
www.healthyminds.org/multimedia/
teensuicide.pdf.

William T. Basco
Jr.

"Teens at Risk: A Focus on
Adolescent Suicide," *Medscape Today*,
2006. www.medscape.com/
viewarticle/540353.

Index